Substance Use & Alcohol
A MyMSW.info Field Guide

Harvey Norris, MSW, LCSW
&
Daniel Knippel, MSW, LCSW, CAP

1st Edition
TURTLE PRESS

©2013-2014
Harvey Norris & Daniel Knippel

All Rights Reserved
No Part of this book may be reproduced, stored in a retrieval system, or transmitted, in any form or by any means without written permission of the author.

ISBN: 978-1495372094

Printed in the USA
Library of Congress Cataloging in Publication Data

Norris, Harvey S.
Knippel, Daniel

The Scope of This Work!

This work was written to provide a basic introduction to Substance Use Disorders and Alcohol. As MSW's our CSWE accredited programs lack a robust training set in Substance Use issues. Most of your training in substance use will come at the postgraduate level. You will be, or have been, amazed at the number of your clients who are substance involved. This work is designed to help you overcome that knowledge/skills gap.

This may be your first introduction to substance use treatment, but it should certainly not be your last. Explore, read and participate in treatment. You will be amazed at the number of other professionals in the field, which will be happy to share their training, education and professional experience with you.

Above all, never be afraid to ask for help or more information.

Sincerely,

Harvey Norris   Daniel Knippel

How This Work is Organized:

This is a field guide! It can be read front to back, back to front, or you can skip around to the lessons and information you find interesting. It is combined with a post-test that can be accessed at www.mymsw.info and can be used to earn 9 CEU's for continuing education as an LCSW in any jurisdiction which allows distance education and accepts the credentialing in Florida.

Carry it with you!

Leave it on your desk as a reference!

Throw it in your briefcase or purse!

Just don't put it on a shelf and let it gather dust!

Learn, Live, Prosper!

But most of all enjoy!

This book is dedicated to:

All the Social Workers and Addiction Therapists who have to shoulder the responsibility of providing treatment, usually without adequate recognition, resources or compensation.

Table of Contents

Lesson 1	Starting with the Facts:	7
Lesson 2	Let's start with some definitions:	11
Lesson 3	Psychological And Socio-Environmental Risk Factors Models	16
Lesson 4	Known Risk Factors For Alcohol Dependence	21
Lesson 5	Alcohol Dependence	26
Lesson 6	Alcohol Dependence VS. Alcohol Abuse VS. the C.A.G.E.	31
Lesson 7	Withdrawal & Tolerance	36
Lesson 8	Preoccupation with Alcohol	43
Lesson 9	Physical Clues That May Suggest Alcohol Abuse Or Dependence -- PART 1 of 2	47
Lesson 10	Physical Clues That May Suggest Alcohol Abuse Or Dependence -- PART 2 of 2	52
Lesson 11	Complications Arising From Alcohol Abuse & Dependence	59
Lesson 12	COMPLICATIONS - Physical disorders are associated with Alcohol Use.	63
Lesson 13	COMPLICATIONS – Part 2	67
Lesson 14	COMPLICATIONS – Part 3	72
Lesson 15	COMPLICATIONS – Part 4	78
Lesson 16	COMPLICATIONS – Part 5	82
Lesson 17	Alcohol and its problems	87
Lesson 18	Brief Intervention	92
Lesson 19	Substance Abuse treatment is effective!	98
Lesson 20	ALCOHOLICS ANONYMOUS	105
Lesson 21	Motivational Interviewing Defined…	112
Lesson 22	Part of the beauty of Motivational Interviewing is its complex interconnections.	119
Lesson 23	One of the primary acronyms used in MI is O.A.R.S.	127
Lesson 24	What MI is…	133
Appendix A		142
References		146

Real World with Dan Knippel

Self-Reevaluation	10
Your client says he is ready to quit using drugs, but his roommate continues to use.	15
Your client, Joe, just arrived for his third session.	19
Make a List of the Good and Not So Good	24
Justification	29
Basic Clinical Skill #1: Acknowledge	34
Expect Substance Abusers To Minimize How Much They Use.	41
Basic Clinical Skill #2: Validate	45
Basic Clinical Skill #3: Complimenting	50
Raising Awareness: The CHAIN of Behaviors That Lead to Drug and Alcohol Use	57
Seriously, Just Say No	61
Excessive Free Time: The Enemy of Abstinence.	65
When Progress Stalls: Keeping receipts & examining yearly totals.	70
Awareness + Behavior Change = Success	75
Excessive Free Time: The Enemy of Abstinence. Part 2,	80
What if a client wants to stop treatment too soon?	85
Avoid asking "Why?"	90
What if your client needs inpatient treatment but has no way of paying for it?	96
Clients often blame the treatment program for failing them, saying, "it" did not work.	103
Do past substance abusers make better substance abuse counselors?	110
Measuring treatment success using a simple, custom assessment questionnaire.	117
The Treatment Plan	125
Searching for Strengths	131
Resist the Urge to Be the Expert.	140

Substance Use & Alcohol
www.MyMSW.info

Lesson # 1

Starting with the Facts:

People drink for many reasons. An exhaustive list of why people drink is beyond the scope of this work. We will examine what are usually considered the "major reasons" people drink alcohol paired with possible needs they are trying to meet. These include:

Reason:	Need:
The pleasurable feeling that often accompanies drinking	Escape, Freedom, seeking pleasure
Reduced tension and anxiety	Escape, social interaction, burden relief
Enjoyment of the Social inclusion	Affiliation, Belonging, Acceptance
Self-medication	Control, Autonomy, Order
Peer pressure	Affiliation, Avoidance of Shame
Behavioral and physical addiction	Physiology

[DHHS 2010]

The statistics are eye-opening. Roughly 90% of adults in the United States have had some experience with alcohol.
[Schuckit 2000]

Alcohol Use:
According to the DHHS National Survey of 2010, roughly half of all Americans 12-years-old and older report being current consumers of

alcohol. Almost 1 in 4 Americans participated in binge drinking at least once in the 30 days prior to the survey. College graduates use alcohol at higher rates than those with only a high school diploma (68.4% and 35.2%, respectively). Roughly 17 million Americans, age 12 and older, report being heavy drinkers.

Binge Drinking:
Binge drinking is defined as episodic, excessive drinking. While there is no World-Wide consensus on the number of drinks it takes to create a "binge", in The United States there is a colloquial definition called the "5/4 definition". It means males who consume more than 5 drinks at one seating or females who drink more than 4 drinks at a time.

Binge drinking by race, according to the DHHS National Survey, in America breaks down as follows...

    11.1% for Asians
    19.8% for Blacks
    22.2% for American Indians or Alaska Natives
    24.1% for persons reporting two or more races
    24.8% for Whites
    25% for Hispanics.

Binge drinking is also associated with an increased risk of unplanned sex, unprotected sex, unplanned pregnancies, and an increased risk of HIV infection. It is important to note that 10 percent of women and 19 percent of men have reported being assaulted as a result of alcohol. Approximately 16 percent of binge drinkers report being taken advantage of sexually, and 8 percent report taking advantage of another person sexually.

Males who drink more than 35 units of alcohol per week report being physically hurt (Self-Damage) as a result of alcohol and their drinking, and 15 percent report physically hurting others (Assault and Battery) as a result of their drinking.

Alcohol Related problems:
About 40 percent of people who drink have experienced an alcohol-related problem. [Schuckit 2000]

Roughly 3-8 percent of women will become alcohol dependent at some point in their lives and roughly 10-15 percent of men will become alcohol dependent at some point in their lives.

Also, repeated intoxication at an early age increases the risk of developing an alcohol use disorder. Dependence usually develops between the mid-twenties and the age of forty. [DHHS 2010]

"Self-Reevaluation"

Your client is at the point where he expresses regret or guilt over his drug or alcohol use. Use this as a time to increase awareness and increase motivation to change.

PROBLEM:

Your client has been abusing drugs or alcohol and is saying to you that he has regrets about that use.

WHAT YOU CAN DO:

Acknowledge and reflect what your client says. Keep your client talking about why it is important for him to change. "What you have been doing doesn't match what you want to be doing. You have higher standards for yourself and you're ready to start the next chapter of your life."

DESIRED OUTCOME:

Listen to see if the client is ready to start talking about change. He may respond with something like, "Yes, that's right. I feel like I haven't done anything with my life." To which you reflect and then test to see if he is ready to change. You reply, "For you, using drugs and alcohol is like being stuck in a rut. You're ready to start a better life. I'm curious what step you will take first."

Recognizing and fostering motivation to change is one of the most important roles a therapist has.

Substance Use & Alcohol

www.MyMSW.info

Lesson # 2

Let's start with some definitions:

Tolerance:
(1) a need for markedly increased amounts of the substance to achieve intoxication or desired effect; or
(2) a markedly diminished effect with continued use of the same amount of the substance [DSM IV 1994].

Standard Drink:
A shot of liquor, a glass of wine, or a can of beer
(1.5 ounces of 80-proof distilled spirits, 5 ounces of table wine, or 12 ounces of beer) [Doufor, 1999].

Alcohol Intoxication:
Maladaptive behaviors or psychological changes (e.g., inappropriate sexual or aggressive behavior, mood changes, impaired judgment, and impaired social or work behavior) that result from recent alcohol consumption [DSM IV 1994].

Changes include slurred speech, loss of coordination, unsteady walking or running, impairment of attention or memory, nystygmus (rhythmic, oscillating motions of the eyes), stupor, or coma.

Alcohol Withdrawal:
The presence of certain symptoms after stopping or reducing heavy and prolonged alcohol use [DSM IV 1994].

The symptoms of alcohol withdrawal may develop within a few hours to a few days after stopping or reducing use and symptoms cause significant physical and emotional distress in social, work, or other important areas of functioning.

Symptoms include increased hand tremor, sweating, increased pulse rate, nausea, vomiting, insomnia, temporary hallucinations or illusions, anxiety, psychomotor agitation, and grand mal seizures.

Fewer than 5% of persons who develop alcohol withdrawal experience severe symptoms such as seizures and death. [Trevisan 1998]

Blood Alcohol Concentration (BAC):
The percentage of alcohol present in the bloodstream. The BAC is usually what is measured by law enforcement to determine legal intoxication. It can be measured directly from a blood sample or a breath sample collected by a "Breathalyzer."

Moderate Drinking:
No more than one drink per day for women and no more than two drinks per day for men [USDA 2000].

Current Use:
At least one drink in the past 30 days. [DHHS 2010]

Binge Drinking:
Consuming five or more drinks on the same occasion in the past 30 days [DHHS 2010].

Heavy Drinking:
Five or more drinks on the same occasion on each of 5 or more days in the past 30 days [DHHS 2010].

Fetal alcohol Syndrome (FAS):
A lifelong syndrome in children with confirmed prenatal exposure to alcohol. Signs include growth deficiencies, facial abnormalities, and neurocognitive deficits that may lead to problems with vision, hearing, attention, learning, memory, or any combination thereof [Bertrand 2004].

The Study:
In a 2002 study of alcohol use involving 14,000 students on college campuses, Harvard University researchers reported 31 percent met the

criteria for alcohol abuse and another 6 percent met the criteria for diagnosis of alcohol dependence [Knight 2002].

The study defined alcohol abuse as:
A positive response to any one of the four abuse criteria and the absence of dependence.
> (1) recurrent alcohol use resulting in a failure to fulfill major role obligations at work, school, or home (e.g., repeated absences or poor work performance related to alcohol use; alcohol-related absences, suspensions, or expulsions from school; neglect of children or household)
> (2) recurrent alcohol use in situations in which it is physically hazardous (e.g., driving an automobile or operating a machine when impaired by alcohol use)
> (3) recurrent alcohol-related legal problems (e.g., arrests for alcohol-related disorderly conduct)
> (4) continued alcohol use despite having persistent or recurrent social or interpersonal problems caused or exacerbated by the effects of the alcohol (e.g., arguments with spouse about consequences of Intoxication, physical fights)

The study defined Alcohol Dependence as:

A positive response to any three or more of seven dependence criteria.

(1) Tolerance, as defined by either of the following:
> (a) a need for markedly Increased amounts of alcohol to achieve Intoxication or desired effect
> (b) markedly diminished effect with continued use of the same amount of alcohol

(2) Withdrawal, as manifested by either of the following:
> (a) the characteristic withdrawal syndrome for alcohol (refer to Criteria A and B of the criteria sets for Withdrawal from alcohol)
> (b) alcohol (or a closely related drug such as valium) is used to relieve or avoid withdrawal symptoms

(3) alcohol is often used in larger amounts or over a longer period than was intended

(4) there is a persistent desire or unsuccessful efforts to cut down or control alcohol use
(5) a great deal of time is spent in activities necessary to obtain alcohol, use alcohol, or recover from its effects
(6) important social, occupational, or recreational activities are given up or reduced because of alcohol use
(7) alcohol use is continued despite knowledge of having a persistent or recurrent physical or psychological problem that is likely to have been caused or exacerbated by alcohol (e.g. continued drinking despite recognition that an ulcer was made worse by alcohol consumption)

Male students are at greater risk than females.
Almost 10 percent of male students and 5 percent of female college students younger than 24 years of age met the criteria for a 12-month diagnosis of alcohol dependence [Knight 2002]

Your client says he is ready to quit using drugs, but his roommate continues to use. Many times, this sets him up for failure because he will be around "unsafe people" who are using.

PROBLEM: Your client wants to quit but his roommate still uses.

WHAT YOU CAN DO:
>"So, it sounds like you are ready to end your relationship with the drug. But I'm curious, how easy will it be for you to end your relationship with the drug if your roommate keeps bringing it home every night?"

DESIRED OUTCOME:
>Expect your client to respond, "Yeah, I wouldn't want my girlfriend coming over all the time after we broke up. Either my roommate has to stop or I have to find another place the live."
>
>The goal is to try to guide the client to the decision that the roommate is an unsafe person and he needs to change his living situation. Don't be confrontational; have the client be his own confronter. The client knows the roommate is going to keep reminding him of the "relationship" he had with the drug. Using humor and the relationship analogy means the client can see that, like a breakup with a romantic partner, if the "ex" keeps coming around all the time (or starts dating your roommate) the breakup will be more difficult.
>Fostering motivation to change is one of the most important roles a therapist has.

Substance Use & Alcohol
www.MyMSW.info

Lesson # 3

Psychological and Socio-Environmental Risk Factors Models

Researchers who study risk factors have developed models of how known risk factors may interact to create pathways in children that lead to alcohol dependence.

Model 1: Children With Conduct Problems:

One model focuses on children who have temperaments that make it difficult for them to regulate their emotions and control their impulses.

Children with conduct problems are difficult to parent. If one or both of the parents have a problem with alcohol, it increases the possibility that the children will be poorly socialized and have trouble getting along in school [Cadoret 1995].

Poor academic performance and mainstream peer rejection at school:

Increases the risk for these children to join peer groups where drinking and other risky behaviors are encouraged.

Alcoholic parents are more likely to provide supervision and monitoring for these children, which increases the risks the parents will lose control over them at an early age.

These children will begin drinking early, often before 15 years of age [Grant 2001].

If such a child is genetically predisposed to alcohol dependence, these environmental factors may further increase the tendency [Goodwin 1974].

Model 2: Stress and Distress:

Another model of risk factors leading to alcohol dependence focuses on drinking to regulate inner distress [Conrod 1995].

> **Point #1:** Some children have temperaments that make them highly reactive to stress and disruption.
>
> **Point #2:** This type of child may be born into an alcoholic family, where the stressors may be intense, or a nonalcoholic family, with everyday types of low-level stressors.
>
> **Point #3:** Regardless of the child's family environment, he or she maintains higher levels of inner distress (anxious and depressed feelings) than other children.

Result: When they take their first drink, the inner distress dissipates for a while. This leads (through behavioral conditioning and positive reinforcement) to more drinking and increases the risk of leading to alcohol dependence.

However, for some individuals, at certain doses, alcohol may induce rather than reduce the stress response.
Research demonstrates that alcohol actually induces the stress response by stimulating hormone release by the hypothalamus, pituitary, and adrenal glands [Soderpalm 2002].

More research is required before the role of stress as a risk factor in alcohol dependence is understood.

Model 3: Sensitivity to Alcohol's Effects:

This risk factor model focuses on sensitivity to the effects of alcohol, both to its sedative properties and its stimulating qualities [Volavka 1996].

The stimulant-like (increased heart rate and blood pressure) and sedative properties (impaired vigilance and psychomotor performance) depend on the quantity of alcohol consumed, the time elapsed since consumption, and individual differences in response [Holdstock 1998; 2001].

Volavka and colleagues found that low electroencephalogram response to small amounts of alcohol might be associated with future development of alcohol dependence.

In another study, Biphasic alcohol response
Heavy drinkers had less sedation and cortisol response after alcohol consumption than light drinkers. [Holdstock 1998]

In addition:
Heavy drinkers were more sensitive to the positive stimulant-like properties as blood alcohol levels increased [King 2002].

The Real World Scenario:
Your client, Joe, just arrived for his third session. During the first two sessions, Joe said, "I want to put drinking behind me" and, "I don't want to drink when I'm upset or drink to get drunk anymore." Joe said he drinks an average of 12 beers per day. He buys a 6-pack of beer on the way home, and then goes out for another 6-pack later in the evening. Today, Joe admitted that last week he still drank his usual 6-pack of beer after work, but he smiles when he tells you that the last four days he only bought an additional quart of beer, not the usual second 6-pack. He said, "I'm trying."

> Does Joe seem proud of the small reduction in drinking or is he frustrated that it is not a bigger reduction?
>
> Is Joe progressing fast enough for you?
>
> What "Stage of Change" is Joe currently in?

"I'll be able to have just one or two"

Your client has a long history of daily alcohol dependence with significant problems caused by alcohol. He says he wants to quit, but then he backtracks and says he thinks he can get to the point where he just has a "couple drinks, but I won't get drunk".

PROBLEM:
Your client is afraid to commit to abstinence. His relationship with substances is so strong that he hesitates when faced with thoughts of "breaking off" the relationship for good.

WHAT YOU CAN DO:
First, reflect what your client says he wants to do. "You would like to be able to drink just a couple drinks at special occasions or dinner and not have it end up causing problems."

Try humor:
> "Although… and correct me if I'm wrong…"
> "You mentioned a whole list of problems linked with drinking alcohol."
> "You felt alcohol had control over you, not the other way around."
> "So… I guess it makes perfect sense to keep drinking?"

Or try an amplified reflection:
> "You don't see any reason not to keep drinking."

(Read about Motivational Enhancement Therapy for an explanation of Amplified Reflections)

DESIRED OUTCOME:
Your client might nod and say: "Sure, I get it. You're saying that if I want to quit then I should go ahead and quit instead of trying to find excuses to still drink."

> *(Your goal in treatment is to always guide the client. You are never responsible for whether they drink or not. You are never trying to SAVE them!)*

The goal is to try to guide the client to the decision to quit.
The goal is to get him to say it, not you. If he says that he should quit, he owns it and it has more power than if his therapist (or anybody else) tells him he should quit. Remember, guide your clients to their own solution, and don't push them to it.

A therapist should rarely offer advice. Instead, the therapist poses a dilemma meant to make the client deal with their ambivalence between drinking or not drinking. You want the client to settle his own doubt by hearing him say something like, "Nah, I'd better not keep drinking, it's not safe for me to drink." Don't tell him not to drink, have him tell himself.

Substance Use & Alcohol
www.MyMSW.info

Lesson # 4

Known Risk Factors For Alcohol Dependence

Remember the three models we learned about in Issue #4 (Children With Conduct Problems, Stress and Distress, and Sensitivity to Alcohol's Effects)?

With these three models in mind, a review of some of the research findings on genetic and psychosocial risk factors may provide a better understanding of the factors leading to alcohol dependence [Schuckit 2000, Sullivan 2001].

Temperament:
Moodiness, negativity, and provocative behavior may lead to a child being criticized by teachers and parents. These strained adult-child interactions may increase the chances that a child will drink.

Hyperactivity:
Hyperactivity in childhood is a risk factor for the development of adult alcohol dependence.
Children with attention deficit hyper-activity disorder (ADHD) and conduct disorders have increased risk of developing an alcohol use disorder.

Childhood aggression also may predict adult alcohol abuse. Research shows parents to be the most important factor in an adolescent's decision to drink.

Gender:
Among adults, heavy alcohol use is almost three times more common among men than women and also more common among males in middle or high school than among females.

Males with ADHD and/or conduct disorders are more likely to use alcohol than males without these disorders, while females who experience more depression, anxiety, and social avoidance as children are more likely to begin using alcohol as teens than females who do not experience these negative states.

Psychology:
Bipolar disorder, schizophrenia, antisocial personality disorder, and panic disorder all also increase the risk of a future alcohol use disorder.

Abuse And Adverse Conditions In The Home
Childhood abuse is a significant risk factor for later alcohol and substance abuse [Schuck 2001].

Women who were physically abused are 1.5 to 2 times more likely to abuse alcohol than non-abused adults.

Children from crowded, noisy, and disorderly homes without rules or religion are more likely to abuse alcohol as teens.

Children who are quick to anger, who perceive themselves to be highly stressed, who are resentful of parents' absences, or who have repeated conflicts at home are more likely to abuse alcohol as teens.

Protective Factors

An exciting area of research is currently focused on protective factors and poses the question, "What protects children from taking one of the risk pathways to alcohol dependence?"

In 1997, some good news came from the National Longitudinal Study on Adolescent Health, a survey in which nearly 12,000 students in grades 7 through 12 were given lengthy interviews timed one year apart.

The researchers were trying to determine what kept children, over the course of that year, from taking health risks in four areas: substance abuse (cigarettes, alcohol, and marijuana), sexuality, violence, and emotional health [Resnick 1997].

The researchers found two factors that protected these children in all four areas.

They named the factors:
Parent-family connectedness and school connectedness. Children identified as having parent-family connectedness said they felt close to their mother or father, felt that their mother or father cared about them, felt satisfied with their relationship with their mother or father, and felt loved by family members [Resnick 1997].

School connectedness was experienced as a feeling of being part of one's school and a belief that students were treated fairly by the teachers.

ACTIVITY:
Make a List of the Good and Not So Good

PROBLEM:
Drug and alcohol users will rationalize their own substance abuse by using a wide array of excuses. They often minimize risks and problems and maximize anything that supports their desire to keep using. Among other things, users may say:

    1) everybody does it,
    2) I'm not hurting anybody,
    3) it's legal in other states and it's used as medicine so it's not a big deal,
    4) alcohol is worse or,
    5) at least I'm not popping pills, or,
    6) I know this guy who's been using for years and he's successful.

It is important to recognize this as the Pre-Contemplation Stage of the Stages of Change Model (also called the Transtheoretical Model).

At the Pre-Contemplation Stage, your job as a counselor is to have the client begin to explore any ambivalence about his own excuses.

WHAT YOU CAN DO: The Good and Not So Good activity.

On a piece of paper, make two lists. On the left, have the client list the Good things about using drugs and alcohol. Be honest, substances can make us feel good and relieve stress or help us sleep, among other things.

Then, on the right side of the paper, have the client make a list of the things about using drugs and alcohol that are Not So Good. Try to cover all aspects of life: school, work, finances, family relationships, friendships, romantic relationships, legal consequences, health, physical danger, long term effects, mental health, etc.

The Not So Good list is usually the longest.

Next, compare the two lists.

> What is the client aware of about his life?
> What is the client aware of about his morals?
> What is the client aware of about his standards?
> What is the client aware of about how his behavior affects others?

DESIRED OUTCOME:
This exercise is valuable and can produce modest change in attitude. Clients might say something like, "OK, I see that I am just making excuses for something that's not really that good for me." You are successful when the client begins to doubt the validity of their excuses to use drugs and alcohol.

Unfortunately, some clients, especially adolescents, can be stubborn about changing. Young people have sometimes not been impacted enough from their choices to make the absolute best use of the Not So Good list. This exercise usually works well with adults.

When someone is in Pre-Contemplation your job is to guide them toward a change in attitude about their harmful choices.
A counselor should avoid telling the client what to do and how to think. It is more powerful if the client convinces himself to change his own attitude.

Substance Use & Alcohol
www.MyMSW.info

Lesson # 5

Alcohol Dependence

Alcohol dependence is a chronic, primary disease. It is progressive and often fatal. It is NOT a symptom of another physical or mental condition. It is a disease all by itself. Just like heart disease, lung disease and cancer, it has a very clear set of easily definable symptoms that are shared by all people who have the disease.

Roughly 16 million Americans meet the DSM-IV criteria for ALCHOL ABUSE or ALCOHOL DEPENDENCE. That works out to one-in-twenty Americans. When you are standing at your kids school surrounded by 300 parents, you know 15 of them will probably die from this disease.

In addition there are more than 3 million Americans at any time abusing or dependent on illicit or illegal drugs while using alcohol. [SAMSHA 2009].

Just like heart disease, lung disease and cancer, alcohol dependence progresses and can worsen over time. People who suffer from alcohol dependence watch their lives and relationships change. They experience emotional and physical changes in their relationships with their family, co-workers and community. If they do not receive treatment specifically targeted to alcohol dependence, these changes continue towards a devastating finale.

Alcohol dependence leads to premature death through overdose, through brain damage, liver damage, heart damage as well as damage to many other organ systems.

Alcohol Dependence and excessive alcohol consumption are correlated with suicide, motor vehicle accidents, criminal charges, domestic violence and other traumatic issues.

Alcohol dependence, when left untreated can result in the complete destruction of the patient's family, support structures, employment opportunities and their freedom through incarceration for criminal behavior.

As noted, alcohol problems can often be prevented by early identification and brief intervention. A weak link in the early identification of problems is the lack of skill and competencies necessary to perform such an assessment and the experience to confidently move to more specific questions and suggestions for change.

Clinical Symptoms include:

- Development of tolerance to the effects of alcohol
    (i.e., the individual requires more alcohol to achieve the desired effects)
- Experience of withdrawal symptoms
    (e.g., tremors, rapid heartbeat, delirium when alcohol is not available or when intake is reduced)
- Impaired control over drinking
    (e.g., the individual is unable to stop drinking when they want to.)
- Preoccupation with obtaining or consuming alcohol
    (e.g., the individual thinks about drink even when they are in situations where they cannot drink.)
- Continued use of alcohol despite adverse consequences
    (e.g., uses alcohol even after being arrested, fired, divorced, sanctioned)
- Distortions in thinking, most notably denial
    (e.g., individual exhibits a complete refusal to acknowledge their behavior.)

Healthcare professionals must understand the criteria and warning signs of alcohol dependence. This enables the healthcare professional to confront the patient and begin intervention early in the course of this disease instead of waiting for toxic liver markers.

The healthcare professional must then perform an office intervention, if possible, which consists of
> 1) verifying the facts that show a person is at risk for alcohol dependence and
> 2) confronting individual with those facts.

Brief intervention is most effective before alcohol dependence is reached.

Once a patient is diagnosed with alcohol dependence, the need for referral to a more comprehensive and possibly residential program is needed.

Justification

Your client is on his eighth counseling session. He is on probation and is facing a three-year prison sentence if he violates. He failed a urine drug screening for cannabis last week. He admitted that he smoked marijuana to cope after he got mad at a coworker. He justified his drug use by saying, "I got high so that I didn't do something stupid and hurt that guy at work. Then I would really be in trouble if I got another battery charge."

Today, your client said if he gets caught by probation for the failed urine drug screening and has to go to prison, he still made the better of two bad choices.

How would you respond to your client's statement that he did the right thing by using drugs to cope with his anger?

Drug use versus anger: which is the more important concern to your client?

The Drug and Alcohol Relationship: *The Relationship Analogy*

As a counselor, you will build a collection of "scripts" that help you reframe concepts so clients can understand them easily in real-world terms. Here is one of them.

THE PROBLEM:

Substance abusers often use drugs and alcohol to cope with problems. Over time, some people get high so they don't have to cope or deal with their human problems. The drug or alcohol becomes a friend that reliably (although only temporarily) reduces feelings of stress or worry and delays the need to honestly attend to human relationships (Nakken, 1988, 1996).

WHAT YOU CAN DO:
Take some time to discuss substance use using the Relationship Analogy. You might say, "Remember when you first started dating someone, how wonderful it felt? Remember the butterflies in your stomach? And it's true, that just like a relationship, the drug is giving you what you want for a while and it makes you feel good and you really like it and you believe it likes you back."

You continue to explain the relationship connection and say, "When you started using the drug, you learned the effect it had on you. Over time, you learned that when things weren't working out with your human relationships you could go to the drug and you knew what you were going to get. It becomes like a relationship."

You continue to explain, "However, like many relationships, if there are problems they don't stay hidden forever. There comes a time when things don't look so good and we start to notice that maybe this isn't the best relationship for me to be in, for whatever reason. So just like a boyfriend or girlfriend, you might try to break up, only to find yourself getting back together again. Then, a little while later, you break up again because of the same Not So Good* problems that made you want to break up in the first place. You might break up over and over again before you move on for good."

Ask your client, "How is your use like a relationship?"

DESIRED OUTCOME:
Your client might respond with something like, "I never thought of it that way but that is exactly what it's like." Clients usually enjoy this analogy. This is a simple and unique way to reframe their efforts to reach sobriety.

TIP: In future sessions, ask your clients, "How's the breakup going?"

*See the Good and Not As Good activity on Page 26.

Substance Use & Alcohol
www.MyMSW.info

Lesson # 6

Alcohol Dependence VS. Alcohol Abuse VS. the C.A.G.E.

Alcohol Dependence (Alcoholism) and alcohol abuse are two different forms of problem drinking.

Alcoholism is when you have signs of physical addiction to alcohol and continues to drink, despite problems with physical health, mental health, and social, family, or job responsibilities. Alcohol may control your life and relationships.

Alcohol abuse is when drinking leads to problems, but not physical addiction.

How much you drink can influence your chances of becoming dependent. Those at risk for developing alcoholism include:

- Men who have 15 or more drinks a week
- Women who have 12 or more drinks a week
- Anyone who has five or more drinks per occasion at least once a week

Drink Defined:
One drink is defined as a 12-ounce bottle of beer, a 5-ounce glass of wine, or a 1 1/2-ounce shot of liquor.

Your Client's Risk:
You have an increased risk for alcohol abuse and dependence if you have a parent with alcoholism.

You may also be more likely to abuse alcohol or become dependent if you:

- Are a young adult under peer pressure
- Have depression, bipolar disorder, anxiety disorders, or schizophrenia
- Have easy access to alcohol

- Have low self-esteem
- Have problems with relationships
- Live a stressful lifestyle
- Live in a culture alcohol use is more common and accepted

Symptoms:
People who have Alcoholism or Alcohol Abuse often:
- Continue to drink, even when health, work, or family are being harmed
- Drink alone
- Become violent when drinking
- Become hostile when asked about drinking
- Are not able to control drinking -- being unable to stop or reduce alcohol intake
- Make excuses to drink
- Miss work or school, or have a decrease in performance because of drinking
- Stop taking part in activities because of alcohol
- Need to use alcohol on most days to get through the day
- Neglect to eat or eat poorly
- Do not care about or ignore how they dress or whether they are clean
- Try to hide alcohol use
- Shake in the morning or after periods when they have not had a drink

Symptoms of Alcohol Dependence include:
- Memory lapses after heavy drinking
- Needing more and more alcohol to feel "drunk"
- Alcohol withdrawal symptoms when you haven't had a drink for a while
- Alcohol-related illnesses such as alcoholic liver disease

Welcome to the CAGE Questionnaire:
A Screening Test for Alcohol Dependence

In just four questions, the CAGE simple self-test has proven accurate in identifying usage patterns that reflect problems with alcohol dependence. The test specifically focuses on the use of alcohol.

1. Have you ever felt you should <u>cut</u> down on your drinking?
☐ Yes ☐ No
2. Have people <u>annoyed</u> you by criticizing your drinking?
☐ Yes ☐ No
3. Have you ever felt bad or <u>guilty</u> about your drinking?
☐ Yes ☐ No
4. Have you ever had a drink first thing in the morning to steady your nerves or get rid of a hangover (<u>eye</u>-opener)?
☐ Yes ☐ No

The CAGE questionnaire was developed by Dr. John Ewing, founding director of the Bowles Center for Alcohol Studies, University of North Carolina at Chapel Hill.

CAGE is an internationally used assessment instrument for identifying problems with alcohol. 'CAGE' is an acronym formed from the underlined words in the questionnaire (cut-annoyed-guilty-eye).

Basic Clinical Skill #1:

Acknowledge

As a counselor, you will likely have a handful of techniques you use over and over in your practice. For example, you might like to have clients use art in therapy or you might encourage most of your clients to journal.

However, there are a few core clinical skills that everyone should know and use. Three of the core skills to know are:
    1) acknowledging,
    2) validating, and
    3) complimenting.

Acknowledging is the art of letting the client know you heard them. (Similar to *reflections* in Motivational Enhancement.)

THE PROBLEM:

Although it should be a requirement, not every counselor does a good job at the simple but primary task of acknowledging a client's concerns. Too many counselors offer advice too quickly, trying the be the expert. Read the following scenario and choose the best answer that is the *first* thing a counselor should say.

QUESTION #1:

This is Mr. Smith's fourth session for the presenting problem of alcohol abuse. He tells his therapist, "I have been keeping a secret from my wife. For about three months I have been smoking crack cocaine with my neighbor. I haven't told anyone until now. Every day I tell myself to stop but I just can't."

    a. "Are you going to tell your wife?"

  b. "You should start planning how you're going to say no to your neighbor."
  c. "Do you think you need residential treatment or will outpatient treatment be enough?"
  d. "You're really worried about it...and the secret has been a burden."

QUESTION #2:
A woman is lying alone in a hospital bed, bandaged after being stabbed two days ago by her husband who is now in jail. You, the hospital social worker, are instructed to evaluate the patient's needs and assist with her transition from the hospital. What is the *first* thing you should say to the patient?
  a. "Who is your primary care doctor?"
  b. "If you want counseling I can help link you with services."
  c. "Who is coming to pick you up? Where are you going to stay when you leave the hospital?."
  d. "This must be a really difficult time for you and you're worried about a dozen different things."

WHAT YOU CAN DO:
Before you begin any problem solving, make sure you acknowledge the client's problem. Acknowledging the problem is the best way to reassure the client you are listening and you are both on the same page. You may lose credibility if you do not acknowledge. (Answers: D, D)

DESIRED OUTCOME:
Most of the time, when you acknowledge the problem correctly, the client will say: "Yes! That's exactly how I feel".

If the client knows their problem has been heard and acknowledged, they are then better able to move on to problem solving.

When you acknowledge the client's problem first, the client can confirm that you are attending to what is truly concerning to the client at that time, not something you *think* they should be concerned about. You will likely increase rapport and increase the effectiveness of the therapeutic alliance. Acknowledge the problem first.

Substance Use & Alcohol

www.MyMSW.info

Lesson # 7

Withdrawal & Tolerance

Individuals with Alcohol Dependence often experience a severe withdrawal syndrome when they abruptly discontinue use and also when they sharply reduce their alcohol consumption.

Symptoms include:
Sweating, rapid heartbeat, hypertension, tremors, anorexia, insomnia, agitation, anxiety, nausea, and vomiting.

Tremors of the hands are the earliest symptom of alcohol withdrawal.

Hallucinosis, seizures, and delirium tremens (DTs) are the most severe form of alcohol withdrawal. Hallucinosis can occur one or two days after reducing or stopping alcohol use.

While these effects of DTs can be life threatening, all other symptoms will generally resolve themselves regardless of treatment within several days of abstinence.

Some alcoholics report symptoms consisting of irritability, emotional lability, insomnia, and anxiety that last for a few weeks to several months after abstaining.

This is often called the "Dry Drunk" stage and it may have more to do with the emotional withdrawal from the alcohol than any physical withdrawal symptoms.

Increased Tolerance
Tolerance can develop due to long-term heavy drinking.

Tolerance is the body's adaptation to the presence of alcohol. Tolerance requires the drinker to increase amounts of alcohol to feel the same effect.

Our society often admires people for their ability to "hold their drinks." But tolerance may well be an early warning sign of physical dependence on alcohol. During the later stages of alcohol dependence reverse-tolerance occurs. When this happens the individual becomes intoxicated quicker using less alcohol.

Tolerance and withdrawal are the first two *DSM-IV* criteria. You only need 3 of the 7 symptoms to make a diagnosis of alcohol dependence.

Professionals often focus on highly recognizable behaviors associated with alcohol dependence: These are
(1) impaired control over drinking,
(2) preoccupation with alcohol, and
(3) use of alcohol despite adverse consequences.

Impaired Control over Drinking
This occurs when a person is consistently unable to limit the number of occasions when alcohol is used or the amount of alcohol ingested on those occasions.

This often causes damage in their lives. People who are alcohol dependent will express a strong and persistent desire to cut down or stop drinking.

This may work for weeks or a month, but, because alcohol dependence is a <u>chronic, progressive disease</u>, once alcohol dependent patients resume drinking, they usually return to the previous quantities of consumption, with worsening adverse consequences.

THE D.A.S.T.

The Drug Abuse Screening Test (DAST) was developed in 1982 and is still an excellent screening tool.

It is a 28-item self-report scale that consists of items that parallel those of the Michigan Alcoholism Screening Test (MAST). The DAST has "exhibited valid psychometric properties" and has been found to be "a sensitive screening instrument for the abuse of drugs other than alcohol."

Directions: The following questions concern information about your involvement with drugs. Drug abuse refers to (1) the use of prescribed or "over-the-counter" drugs in excess of the directions, and (2) any non-medical use of drugs. Consider the past year (12 months) and carefully read each statement. Then decide whether your answer is YES or NO and check the appropriate space. Please be sure to answer every question.

1. Have you used drugs other than those required for medical reasons?
   ☐ Yes   ☐ No
2. Have you abused prescription drugs?
   ☐ Yes   ☐ No
3. Do you abuse more than one drug at a time?
   ☐ Yes   ☐ No
4. Can you get through the week without using drugs (other than those required for medical reasons)?
   ☐ Yes   ☐ No
5. Are you always able to stop using drugs when you want to?
   ☐ Yes   ☐ No
6. Do you abuse drugs on a continuous basis?
   ☐ Yes   ☐ No
7. Do you try to limit your drug use to certain situations?
   ☐ Yes   ☐ No
8. Have you had "blackouts" or "flashbacks" as a result of drug use?
   ☐ Yes   ☐ No
9. Do you ever feel bad about your drug abuse?
   ☐ Yes   ☐ No
10. Does your spouse (or parents) ever complain about your involvement with drugs?
    ☐ Yes   ☐ No
11. Do your friends or relatives know or suspect you abuse drugs?
    ☐ Yes   ☐ No

12. Has drug abuse ever created problems between you and your spouse?
    ☐ Yes ☐ No
13. Has any family member ever sought help for problems related to your drug use?
    ☐ Yes ☐ No
14. Have you ever lost friends because of your use of drugs?
    ☐ Yes ☐ No
15. Have you ever neglected your family or missed work because of your use of drugs?
    ☐ Yes ☐ No
16. Have you ever been in trouble at work because of drug abuse?
    ☐ Yes ☐ No
17. Have you ever lost a job because of drug abuse?
    ☐ Yes ☐ No
18. Have you gotten into fights when under the influence of drugs?
    ☐ Yes ☐ No
19. Have you ever been arrested because of unusual behavior while under the influence of drugs?
    ☐ Yes ☐ No
20. Have you ever been arrested for driving while under the influence of drugs?
    ☐ Yes ☐ No
21. Have you engaged in illegal activities in order to obtain drugs?
    ☐ Yes ☐ No
22. Have you ever been arrested for possession of illegal drugs?
    ☐ Yes ☐ No
23. Have you ever experienced withdrawal symptoms as a result of heavy drug intake?
    ☐ Yes ☐ No
24. Have you had medical problems as a result of your drug use (e.g., memory loss, hepatitis, convulsions, bleeding, etc.)?
    ☐ Yes ☐ No
25. Have you ever gone to anyone for help for a drug problem?
    ☐ Yes ☐ No

26. Have you ever been in a hospital for medical problems related to your drug use?
    ☐ Yes   ☐ No
27. Have you ever been involved in a treatment program specifically related to drug use?
    ☐ Yes   ☐ No
28. Have you been treated as an outpatient for problems related to drug abuse?
    ☐ Yes   ☐ No

D.A.S.T. Scoring and interpretation:
A score of "1" is given for each YES response, except for items 4,5, and 7, for which a NO response is given a score of "1." Based on data from a heterogeneous psychiatric patient population, cutoff scores of 6 through 11 are considered to be optimal for screening for substance use disorders. Using a cutoff score of 6 has been found to provide excellent sensitivity for identifying patients with substance use disorders as well as satisfactory specificity (e.g. identification of patients who do not have substance use disorders). Using a cutoff score of <11 somewhat reduces the sensitivity for identifying patients with substance use disorders, but more accurately identifies the patients who do not have a substance use disorders. Over 12 is definitely a substance abuse problem. In a heterogeneous psychiatric patient population, most items have been shown to correlate at least moderately well with the total scale scores. The items that correlate poorly with the total scale scores appear to be items 4,7,16,20, and 22.

The Real World
with
Dan Knippel, LCSW

Expect Substance Abusers To Minimize How Much They Use.

Substance abuse and dependence are maintained by *secrets*, *lies*, and *control*. The drug and alcohol user has to keep *secrets* and tell *lies* in order to maintain *control* of what others know about how much they are using and what they are using.

It is rare for a substance-abusing client to be honest about how much they are using.

THE PROBLEM:
During the initial meetings and assessment phase of treatment, substance abusers often minimize how much of a substance they regularly use. Think about it; it is probably embarrassing to admit that one drinks 25 beers a day or smokes marijuana every hour of the day from morning to night.

Clients do not want others to think that they are out of control. Therefore, the substance abuser is unlikely to be truthful, at least at first, about the amount of drugs or alcohol they really use. They need to keep *secrets* and *lie* to be in *control* of what others know.

During the initial assessment, a client might say they only drink "three or four beers a few times per week" or they only smoke marijuana "once a day in the evening, maybe a couple times per week". With such light use, it doesn't seem like much of a problem.

In all likelihood, the client is using much more of the substance but they are not ready to divulge the true extent of their use.

WHAT YOU CAN DO:

Technique:
Try overestimating the client's drug or alcohol use *before the client tells you how much they use.*

For example:
You are completing an initial assessment. The client admits to abusing alcohol and marijuana. You then say, "Many people I work with drink between 20 or 30 drinks in a typical day", or, "Usually, I hear from people who smoke pot throughout the entire day. What's a normal day for you?"

DESIRED OUTCOME:
The client will say something like, "Well, I sure don't drink 30 beers every day…no way. I might get through about 18 beers but not 30!"

The client admitted to 18 beers per day instead of just "three or four". This client might drink even more than 18, but he doesn't feel like he has to minimize too much because the range you gave was so high.

Knowing how much your client is using can help you direct your counseling skills appropriately.

Substance Use & Alcohol
www.MyMSW.info

Lesson # 8

Preoccupation with Alcohol

This is the stage in the disease process where drinking alcohol becomes a central focus in the user's life.

The user will begin to develop a preoccupation with alcohol, which we will define as a "noticeable shift in priorities, with a focus on obtaining and consuming an adequate supply of alcohol."

As the disease progresses, the individual will devote more energy to their alcohol dependence and will divert energy from people, places, and things that were once important to them.

You will begin to see an increase in the amount of time the user devotes to their alcohol use. Their priorities will begin to focus around obtaining alcohol, drinking alcohol, and recovering from the effects of alcohol. This will begin to take a larger amount of time out of their day.

Often at this time they will begin abandoning hobbies and other recreational activities and will appear to only be able to derive pleasure from drinking.

Use of Alcohol Despite Adverse Consequences:
As the disease progresses, drinkers will find it harder to stop using even though they become aware of the adverse consequences of their use. They may begin to understand how their drinking is affecting their life; including problems involving their family, interpersonal issues, spiritual issues, occupational issues, legal problems, and financial trouble.
Alcohol may also cause serious health and psychological problems including anemia, gastritis, liver disease, neurological disorders, and depression.

Denial as a defense mechanism:
Denial is an integral part of the disease of alcohol dependence and a major obstacle to recovery. It is a common mental filter or cognitive distortion, which allows the user to refuse to accept the consequences of their behavior. The deeper the user sinks into the disease state, the more profoundly they will use DENIAL as a means of refusing to accept their losses.

Relapse:
This disease is chronic, and so is likely to happen at different times throughout the life cycle of the individual.

The professional need to understand that relapse is a part of the disease process and alcohol dependence, while being a treatable disease, has no cure. Even after long periods of sobriety, choices and situations can cause the disease to re-occur.

The Real World with Dan Knippel, LCSW

Basic Clinical Skill #2: Validate

As a counselor, you will likely have a handful of techniques you use over and over in your practice. However, there are a few core clinical skills that everyone should know and use. The most basic skills to know are:
1) acknowledging,
2) validating, and
3) complimenting.

Validating is the art of confirming for the client that their feelings about a problem or their response to a situation make sense. There are a couple benefits to using validating statements.

THE PROBLEM:
Substance abusers often use drugs or alcohol to cope with problems. Getting high is an easy and reliable way for a substance abuser to cope with feelings of anger, frustration, rejection, sadness, fear, or disappointment.

Sometimes, your client will come right out and admit, "I got into a fight with my boyfriend over the weekend and I went to my friend's house and got drunk."

Watch out! Your response here could either hurt or help your therapeutic relationship with your client. Do not try to problem-solve, do not offer advice, and don't ask "Why did you drink?" (Asking "Why?" is like being interrogated – bad idea. We will cover that topic in a future edition.)

WHAT YOU CAN DO:
Try saying something like, "Wow, how frustrating that is to have a big argument with a partner. You just wanted to take your mind off things."

The first sentence acknowledges "how frustrating" arguments can be. The second sentence validates the client's desire to seek relief from her frustration.

> (NOTE: You're not letting the client off the hook here. You are first acknowledging and validating her feelings of frustration. You'll get to the problem of using alcohol to cope with her problems a little later in the session. Just make sure you don't pounce on your clients when they mess up.)

DESIRED OUTCOME:
The client will say something like, "That's right. I just needed to get away from him and his attitude." Then the client may add, "Of course, I realize that drinking doesn't really solve the problem and I guess that's why I'm here in therapy". If the client does not say it herself, you can acknowledge and then reflect on the client's goals, "It was a rough day for you. You're searching for ways to cope with those difficult situations without using." (Then maybe you can start talking about that long list of harmful consequences from the Good and Not So Good list or a list of coping strategies from a treatment plan.)

PRACTICE WISDOM:
Sometimes it is inappropriate to validate someone's behavior. What if someone told you they punched a hole in the wall and fractured their finger just because their boyfriend forgot to bring home bananas from the grocery store? You wouldn't respond with, "Well, not bringing home bananas is a huge problem in most relationships. Sure, most people would have punched the wall if someone forgot to bring home bananas." The response does not match the situation and you'll need to explore what else was going on at the time. Always acknowledge the problem first, then validate when it is appropriate.

Substance Use & Alcohol
www.MyMSW.info

Lesson # 9

PART 1 of 2:
Physical Clues That May Suggest Alcohol Abuse Or Dependence

While a strong attachment to alcohol is the hallmark of early dependency, if the patient refuses to acknowledge a problem and no one from home or work helps to confirm the diagnosis, healthcare professionals are often left with nothing more than clinical intuition, resulting in a missed diagnosis.

However, late in the course of alcohol abuse and dependence, physical clues typically become increasingly apparent and suggestive of alcohol abuse and/or dependence. Alcohol abuse and dependence are often referred to as the "Great Masquerader" because many of the signs and symptoms are also commonly found in other conditions.

Elevated laboratory Findings

Serum Glutamic Oxaloacetic Transaminase (SGOT)
An enzyme that is normally present in liver and heart cells. SGOT is released into blood when the liver or heart is damaged.

Lactic Acid Dehydrogenase (LDH)
An enzyme that helps produce energy and becomes elevated in response to cell damage. LDH levels help diagnose lung disease, lymphoma, anemia, and liver disease.

Triglycerides
High triglycerides are usually caused by other conditions, such as: Drinking a lot of alcohol.

Cholesterol Gamma Glutamyl Transferase (GGT)
Elevated GGT can signify many serious health issues. The liver enzyme is a telltale sign of many liver diseases and cancer, alcoholism, pancreas- and kidney-related issues.

Mean Corpuscular Volume (MCV)
A measure of the average red blood cell size that is reported as part of a standard complete blood count.

Alkaline Phosphatase
Measures the amount of the enzyme ALP in the blood. ALP is made mostly in the liver...some conditions cause large amounts of ALP in the blood. These conditions include... damaged liver cells. (www.WebMD.com)

Blood Alcohol Concentration
Blood alcohol content is usually expressed as a percentage of alcohol (generally in the sense of ethanol) in the blood. For instance, a BAC of 0.10 means that 0.10% (one tenth of one percent) of a person's blood, by volume is alcohol. (www.Wikipedia.com)

Uric Acid
High intake of alcohol (ethanol), is a significant cause of hyperuricemia (increased uric acid). Ethanol increases production of uric acid by increasing production of lactic acid, hence "lactic acidosis".

Gastrointestinal Signs/Symptoms
    Nausea
    Vomiting
    Reflux
    Diarrhea
    Gastritis: (Inflammation of the lining of the stomach often caused by excessive alcohol consumption.)

Ulcers
Break in a bodily membrane that keeps an organ of which that membrane is a part from continuing its normal functions

Esophagitis
Inflammation of the esophagus.

Cardiopulmonary Signs/Symptoms
Hypertension (High Blood Pressure)

Palpitations
Palpitations are unpleasant sensations of irregular and/or forceful beating of the heart.

Arrhythmias
Arrhythmias refer to heartbeat rhythms that are too slow, too rapid, or irregular

Streptococcus Pneumonia:
A bacterium that can infect the upper respiratory tract and cause pneumonia.

Recurrent Respiratory Infections:
Drinking alcohol increases the movement of harmful bacteria (Streptococcus pneumoniae) into the lung while smoking cigarettes exacerbates the alcohol-induced increase in the bacterial penetration.

The Real World with Dan Knippel, LCSW

Basic Clinical Skill #3: Complimenting

As a counselor, you will likely have a handful of techniques you use over and over in your practice. However, there are a few core clinical skills that everyone should know and use. The most basic skills to know are:
    1) acknowledging,
    2) validating, and
    3) complimenting.

Complimenting is the art of acknowledging a client's strengths and contributions in a way that makes them feel proud and appreciated. This technique helps strengthen the therapeutic alliance between client and counselor.

THE PROBLEM:
Substance abusers often do not have people in their lives pointing out their strengths and complimenting them on the things they do well. Now they have you, their counselor, to complement their strengths and increase their potential to be successful.

WHAT YOU CAN DO:

Compliment the client on things they do well.

- If the client tells you they care for three children and work full time, you respond, with, "Wait a minute, where is your cape…because that's the stuff super heroes do."

- If your client says they helped a friend, you say, "Wow, they are really lucky to have you. I work with a lot of people and it is rare when a friend steps up to help like that."

- If your client says they were stressed out but did not use drugs to cope, you say with a smile, "Nice work!! See, I thought I could tell you have been working out, building those coping muscles. You're getting strong!"

- If the client follows their treatment plan well, you can say something like, "You know, I work with a lot of people, and you are doing a great job. There are a lot of people out there who could learn a thing or two from you."

- If the client has good manners and uses proper language skills, you might say, "You really present yourself well. You speak clearly and properly. I bet you have high standards for yourself."

Compliment the client when they complete tasks well, help others, do a good job on their treatment plan, meet sobriety goals, show sympathy or empathy for others, start a new sober activity, reconnect with supportive family or friends, take care of their kids or other family, or any situation where you can say, "Good job!".

DESIRED OUTCOME:
Clients, like most everyone else, usually love being complimented. Often, clients will say, "Thank you. No one ever tells me I do a good job..."

Complimenting opens the door for discussion about how the client has strengths that increase their potential to be successful. After a well-placed compliment, your client might tell you, "You know, I really feel like I can quit for good this time."

WARNING:
Do NOT compliment the client's looks or what they are wearing. This technique is not the same as when you compliment a friend. The purpose of the compliment is to raise awareness of strengths the client can use toward their sobriety goals and some compliments can be misinterpreted as flirting. Therefore, do not compliment the client's shoes or their blouse or their new haircut. Save your compliments for something that benefits the client's clinical progress.

Substance Use & Alcohol
www.MyMSW.info

Lesson # 10

PART 2 of 2:
Physical Clues That May Suggest Alcohol Abuse or Dependence

Alcohol abuse and dependence are often referred to as the "Great Masquerader" because many of the signs and symptoms are also commonly found in other conditions.

Central Nervous System (CNS) Signs/Symptoms

Anxiety
A psychological and physiological state characterized by a displeasing feeling of fear and concern.

Insomnia
A sleep disorder in which there is an inability to fall asleep or to stay asleep as long as desired. It is often defined as a positive response to either of two questions: "Do you experience difficulty sleeping?" or "Do you have difficulty falling or staying asleep?"

Memory impairment

How to complete a memory screen:
Tell the client you are going to give then five objects to remember (Apple, Pen, Tie, House, Car). When you have recited the five objects, ask them to repeat them back to you almost immediately. Score 1 point per item, maximum of 5 points. Continue the interview and in three minutes or so ask them to recall the 5 objects by telling you their names. 1 point for each correct, maximum of 5. You have now completed a Quick Memory Screening of "immediate recall " and "short-term recall"

A score of 4-5 on each set would indicate normal recall. Anything less than that would lead you to consider a memory issue is involved.

Depression
A state of low mood and aversion to activity that can have a negative effect on a client's thoughts, behavior, feelings, world view, and physical being.

Irritability
An excessive response to stimuli. The term is used for both the physiological reaction to stimuli and for the pathological, abnormal or excessive sensitivity to stimuli; it is usually used to refer to anger or frustration.

Panic
A sudden sensation of fear which is so strong as to dominate or prevent reason and logical thinking, replacing it with overwhelming feelings of anxiety and frantic agitation consistent with an animalistic fight-or-flight reaction.

Suicide attempt(s)
Suicidal thinking

Behavioral Clues
- Loss of interest in previously favorite activities and people
- Marital and financial problems
- Positive family history for cigarette smoking
- Problems at home and work
- Anger when someone asks about drinking
- Legal difficulties

Miscellaneous Signs/Symptoms
Gout
A medical condition usually characterized by recurrent attacks of acute inflammatory arthritis—a red, tender, hot, swollen joint. The metatarsal-phalangeal joint at the base of the big toe is the most commonly affected (approximately 50% of cases). Elevated levels of uric acid in the blood cause it. The uric acid crystallizes, and the crystals deposit in joints, tendons, and surrounding tissues.

Parotid swelling
Swelling occurs in parotid glands on both sides of the face, giving the appearance of "chipmunk cheeks."

Trauma injuries
- Aches and pains
- Unusual accidents
- Broken bones
- Driving accidents
- Multiple citations, and other problems

Higher than normal scores on screening questionnaires, such as the:
Michigan Alcohol Screening Test (MAST)
THE M.A.S.T.

Michigan Alcohol Screening Test (MAST), Revised
Selzer, M.L. (1971) 'The Michigan Alcoholism Screening Test (MAST): The quest for a new diagnostic instrument', American Journal of Psychiatry, 127:1653-1658.

1. Do you feel you are a normal drinker? ("normal" is defined as drinking as much or less than most other people)
    ☐ Yes   ☐ No
2. Have you ever awakened the morning after drinking the night before and found that you could not remember a part of the evening?
    ☐ Yes   ☐ No
3. Does any near relative or close friend ever worry or complain about your drinking?
    ☐ Yes   ☐ No
4. Can you stop drinking without difficulty after one or two drinks?
    ☐ Yes   ☐ No
5. Do you ever feel guilty about your drinking?
    ☐ Yes   ☐ No
6. Have you ever attended a meeting of Alcoholics Anonymous (AA):
    ☐ Yes   ☐ No
7. Have you ever gotten into physical fights when drinking?
    ☐ Yes   ☐ No
8. Has drinking ever created problems between you and a near relative or close friend?

☐ Yes   ☐ No

9. Has any family member or close friend gone to anyone for help about your drinking?

☐ Yes   ☐ No

10. Have you ever lost friends because of your drinking?

☐ Yes   ☐ No

11. Have you ever gotten into trouble at work because of drinking?

☐ Yes   ☐ No

12. Have you ever lost a job because of drinking?

☐ Yes   ☐ No

13. Have you ever neglected your obligations, family, or work for two or more days in a row because you were drinking?

☐ Yes   ☐ No

14. Do you drink before noon fairly often?

☐ Yes   ☐ No

15. Have you ever been told you have liver trouble, such as cirrhosis?

☐ Yes   ☐ No

16. After heavy drinking, have you ever had delirium tremens (DTs), severe shaking, visual or auditory (hearing) hallucinations?

☐ Yes   ☐ No

17. Have you ever gone to anyone for help about your drinking?

☐ Yes   ☐ No

18. Have you ever been hospitalized because of drinking?

☐ Yes   ☐ No

19. Has your drinking ever resulted in your being hospitalized in a psychiatric ward?

☐ Yes   ☐ No

20. Have you ever gone to any doctor, social worker, clergyman, or mental health clinic for help with any emotional problem in which drinking was part of the problem?

☐ Yes   ☐ No

21. Have you been arrested more than once for driving under the influence of alcohol?

☐ Yes   ☐ No

22. Have you ever been arrested, or detained by an official for a few hours, because of other behavior while drinking?

☐ Yes   ☐ No

Scoring the MAST Test

Score one point if you answered "no" to the following questions: 1 or 4. Score one point if you answered "yes" to the following questions: 2, 3, 5 through 22.

A total score of six or more indicates hazardous drinking or alcohol dependence and further evaluation by a healthcare professional is recommended.

The Real World with Dan Knippel, LCSW

Raising Awareness:

The CHAIN of Behaviors That Lead to Drug and Alcohol Use
Abracadabra!
Drugs and alcohol magically appear!

PROBLEM:

Some clients will frame alcohol or drug use as out of their control; as something that *happens to them* rather than a behavior they choose to do. The chain of behaviors involved in their repetitive drug and alcohol habits escape conscious awareness.

Many drug and alcohol users will say they, "just ended up doing it", as if by magic. They might say, "I was doing really well for a while. Then I had a rough day and the next thing I know I was getting high."

That's like saying, "I felt hungry and the next thing I knew, I had eaten a large pepperoni pizza." It just doesn't happen that way. It requires the completion of many small steps to obtain and eat a fully cooked pizza. There is always a chain of behaviors to complete any task.

WHAT YOU CAN DO:

Educate the client on the chain of behaviors and then use awareness and stopping techniques to interrupt and redirect the behavior. Use an actual length of chain or draw the links of a chain on paper. Then, label each link in the order in which a user would obtain the substance and use it.

    1) getting into the car
    2) driving to get money
    4) calling the dealer
    5) driving to the dealer's neighborhood
    6) meeting the dealer
    7) driving home with the drugs
    8) going into the house carrying the drugs
    9) using

As you can see, obtaining and using drugs or alcohol usually includes a chain of many small behaviors.

If your client is aware of the chain of behaviors, he can break the chain at any time and choose a different behavior.

TRY THIS:
Maybe use a big sheet of paper to draw a map with the client's house, the liquor store, the roads, the bank ATM, and any other visual representation of the chain of behaviors. Let the client see all the opportunities to break the chain.

DESIRED OUTCOME:
Expect your client to agree that there are a number of opportunities to break the chain of drug and alcohol use behaviors. The client will say something like, "So, I guess I could have stopped anytime but I was just going through the motions without thinking about what I was doing."

Then, with his new awareness of how "in control" he is, the client can think about how and where to break the chain next time.

Substance Use & Alcohol

Lesson # 11

Complications Arising From Alcohol Abuse & Dependence:

Physical Problems:

LIVER DISEASE
- Alcohol is metabolized in the liver prior to being eliminated from the body. This makes the liver very vulnerable to alcohol consumption.
- The most common example of LIVER DAMAGE among alcoholics is the manifestation of "fatty liver."
- Among heavy drinkers, the occurrence of "fatty liver" is almost universal.
- Men who have six or more drinks a day and women who have one or two drinks a day have been associated with "fatty deposits in the liver".
- "Fatty liver" may be the first step to the onset of alcoholic cirrhosis or "swelling of the liver."

Alcoholic Hepatitis:
A condition characterized by jaundice, fever, anorexia, and right upper-quadrant pain.

Heavy Drinkers (those drinking a minimum of five or six standard drinks a day) have a 1 in 3 chance of developing alcoholic hepatitis and 1 in 5 chance of developing cirrhosis [NIAAA 1998].

The Survival Rate for heavy drinkers who develop both alcoholic hepatitis and cirrhosis is grim. Six in ten heavy drinkers will be dead in 4 years.

Amount of alcohol to cause damage:

Drinking 12 beers or standard alcohol drinks each day for 20 years has been linked to a 1 in 2 chance or incident rate of liver cirrhosis.

Issues effecting women:
- Women will develop liver disease faster and at lower alcohol levels than men.
- Women have a higher incidence of alcoholic hepatitis & a higher mortality rate from cirrhosis [Hall 1995].

Liver Transplantation:
Cirrhosis due to alcoholic liver disease is the second most common cause for a person to require a liver transplantation.
Chronic Hepatitis C is the leading reason for liver transplantation in the United States [Dhar 1999].

Survival rate after transplantation is very good. After the first three years between 2-3 of 5-6 patients will still be alive after a transplant. [Dhar 1999].

When patients have both alcohol dependence and chronic hepatitis C, they do worse than when both diseases occur independently.

The Real World with Dan Knippel, LCSW

Seriously, Just Say No

PROBLEM:
Saying "no" is a crucial step for many users as they work a plan to distance themselves from substances and other substance users. Unfortunately, alcohol and drug users associate almost exclusively with other users. For many clients, saying "no" to user friends or relatives does not happen easily.

Clients say they are embarrassed to say no and they feel pressured to use when others around them are using.

Therefore, preparing a script for saying "no" and practicing it should be part of a comprehensive substance abuse treatment plan.

WHAT YOU CAN DO:
Help your client prepare a script for saying "no". Then, when your client is in the company of users, all he has to do is say his already-practiced lines.

There are a few different themes of "no" scripts. They include:
1) the forceful use of direct, unambiguous speech,
2) funny excuses,
3) medical excuses, and,
4) excuses from a list of things your client wants to change
   (the Not So Good* list)

1. First, the easiest way to get the dealers and users to go away is for the client to just say no. Still, he needs to say it convincingly. Avoid saying, "Well, I don't know…" Instead, your client should use clear, concise language such as, "Absolutely not. I'm not smoking or using anymore. I'm done. Don't ask me again."

2. If it matches your client's personality, have him come up with a funny or sarcastic way to say no. Kids do well at this. Example: "Do I want to smoke some pot? Ummm, no. I'm allergic to stupidity, plus I'm trying to lose weight." Example: "Well, no, I don't do drugs anymore. Turns out I become a paranoid drug addict and destroy everything good in my life, so, no thanks."

3. Medical excuses are easy. Save face by declining to use due to a medical reason. Example: "No, I don't drink anymore. I'm on meds that my doctor said could really mess me up if I drank. No more for me." Example: "No way, I'm not using crack. My doctor said I'm already prone to strokes so I am not playing around with that."

4. Lastly, use any excuse from the client's life. If the client says he wants to stop because he is letting his family down, he can say, "I don't use any more. My family is really on me, so I'm done." The client might want to keep a job. He can say, "No way! They're drug testing at work and I'm not taking any chances." Money is a big motivator and the client might say, "No, I'm flat broke and need my money for other things. In fact, maybe you could give me some money..."

DESIRED OUTCOME:
The good news is that drug users do not like hanging out with straight people. Soon after your client says "no" a few times, the users will begin to disappear. They will stop calling and stop coming over. Your client will have to find new friends, but that was the point in the first place. Success!

Substance Use & Alcohol
www.MyMSW.info

Lesson # 12

COMPLICATIONS
Physical disorders are associated with alcohol abuse and dependence.

Cardiovascular Disorders
Alcohol has a detrimental effect on the heart, which includes a decreased myocardial contractility (less ability to pump), hypertension (high blood pressure), and also atrial and ventricular arrhythmias (irregular heartbeat.)

Alcohol dependence is related to elevated pulse and blood pressure. When drinking stops, the blood pressure will often return to normal after several days.

People who have 6 or more drinks a day were two times more likely to suffer from hypertension than drinkers who had 2 or less drinks a day or non-drinkers.

Alcohol has a direct toxicity to the striated muscle of the heart. This can lead to Cardiomyopathy or heart tissue death. [Schoppet 2001].

Alcoholic cardiomyopathy is probably more common than we know because there is a general tendency to under-diagnose alcohol dependence in the general population.

The syndrome "holiday heart syndrome" was first described in people, who engage in heavy alcohol consumption, typically on weekends or after holidays, [Menz 1996]. Rhythm disturbances are associated with heavy alcohol consumption.

The most common rhythm disorder associated with heavy alcohol consumption is atrial fibrillation, which usually converts to normal sinus rhythm within 24 hours.

Vitamin Deficiency, Alcohol, and Cardiovascular Disease

It is common to find malnourished alcoholics with liver diseases have been found to have B6 and folate deficiencies. People with alcohol dependence have a number of nutritional problems. Abnormally high plasma levels of the amino acid homocysteine have been shown to be responsible for an increase in the risk of cardiac disease and other vascular issues [Mangoni 2002].

The vitamins folate, B12, and B6 are required for the body to remove homocysteine from cells.

Studies have shown that the lower the concentration of these vitamins, the greater the concentration of homocysteines. Even small increases in homocysteine appear to increase the risk of heart disease.

It needs to also be noted that the average homocysteine levels are twice as high in chronic alcoholics as they are to non-drinkers. Thus, homocysteine may contribute to the cardiovascular complications experienced by many chronic alcoholics. Using B vitamin supplementation can lower cardiovascular risk. [Chambers 2000]

The Real World with Dan Knippel, LCSW

Excessive Free Time:
The Enemy of Abstinence.
Find Things to Do

PROBLEM:
Excessive free time is a common characteristic of many drug and alcohol users. When asked about their hobbies or what they do for recreation, users are likely to say, "I watch a lot of TV" or, "I play video games." Boredom from nothing to do is a primary trigger for continued substance use and relapses.

WHAT YOU CAN DO:
1. First, start with awareness. Get out a day planner or use paper to draw out a day hour-by-hour.
2. Next, have the client identify the times they usually have breakfast, lunch, and dinner and write them in the timeslots.
3. Third, list any routine scheduled activities such as being at work, in school, or picking kids up. Only include things the client does nearly every day because he is obligated or otherwise committed.
4. Then, write down any activities the client does consistently. Maybe he goes to AA meetings every day or he bowls with a team two nights per week. Maybe he has dinner at his mother's house every Thursday from 6:00 to 8:00PM. If not done at least weekly, do not include it.
5. Discuss the hours and hours of empty spaces on the schedule.
6. Finally, explore realistic, timely activities and incorporate them into the treatment plan. Brainstorm about volunteering, joining groups, getting a job, or anything that disrupts the excessive free time and boredom.

DESIRED OUTCOME:
Your client should quickly say, "Well, it looks like I have a lot of free time." or, "I don't do very much compared to most people."

Finally, your client will identify interests he can pursue to fill the hours of free time. The client should think about re-starting hobbies he used to enjoy, playing an instrument, attending AA or NA meetings, or volunteering at a pet shelter or homeless shelter.

Filling the client's calendar with new things to do will provide some structure, promote abstinence, and help avoid relapse.

Your biggest frustration will be those clients who say they would like to do some new activity but never take the necessary steps to get started. If your employer allows it, you may have to spend a session printing, completing, and submitting volunteer forms or taking the client to the admissions department of a school he wants to attend. Think outside the box and outside the office, if possible.

Substance Use & Alcohol
www.MyMSW.info

Lesson # 13

COMPLICATIONS – Part 2:

Alcohol abuse and dependence are often associated with physical disorders and related problems.

Gastrointestinal Disorders
Alcohol and the entire digestive system do not get along. Alcohol will cause irritation and inflammation of swelling of the mucosal lining of the small and large intestines as well as affecting the motility (movement) of the esophagus, stomach, and small bowel [Stermer 2002].

"Alcoholic heartburn" is caused by the esophageal reflux with esophagitis (the inflammation of the esophagus) that commonly occurs with irritation from chronic alcohol abuse.
Short-term and long-term alcohol ingestion are associated with gastritis, erosive gastritis, gastric ulceration, atrophic gastritis, and gastric hemorrhage.

Patients who have undergone gastric bypass surgery for obesity have higher breath-alcohol levels after drinking the same amount as other people. Findings from a small study suggest that it takes much longer for their levels to return to zero [Hagedorn, 2007].

Chronic Pancreatitis:
The constant inflammation of the pancreas is both damaging and painful. Alcohol consumption is the leading cause of chronic pancreatitis. About 70 percent of the cases in the United States are from alcohol abuse.

One of the effects of chronic pancreatitis is the possibility of the development of diabetes or hyperglycemia as a result of the destruction of the eyelet cells in the pancreas caused by alcohol abuse.

Body Weight
Alcohol is full of calories. Roughly 7.1 calories per gram (1 gram of fat contains 9 calories). Some studied have shown that obese patients, obese patients have gained weight when alcohol is added to their diets.

A recent NHANES survey (National Health and Nutrition Examination Survey) found that while drinkers had a higher intake of calories than non-drinkers they tended to have a decrease in body weight.

When chronic heavy drinkers substitute alcohol for food in their diets, they typically lose weight and weigh less than their nondrinking counterparts [Moses 2013].

- Women drinkers had significantly lower body weight than nondrinkers.
- As alcohol intake among men increased, their body weight decreased.

Korsten (1989) found that alcohol inhibits the breakdown of nutrients into usable molecules by decreasing secretion of digestive enzymes from the pancreas.

Feinman (1989) found that alcohol impairs nutrient absorption by damaging the cells lining the stomach and intestines and disabling transport of some nutrients into the blood.

In addition, nutritional deficiencies themselves may lead to further absorption problems. For example, folate deficiency alters the cells lining the small intestine, which in turn impairs absorption of water and nutrients including glucose, sodium, and additional folate (Feinman 1989).

Even if nutrients are digested and absorbed, alcohol can prevent them from being fully utilized by altering their transport, storage, and excretion (Thomson 1992).

Decreased liver stores of vitamin A (Sato 1981), and increased excretion of nutrients such as fat, indicate impaired utilization of nutrients by alcoholics (Feinman 1989).

The Best Way to Treat Malnourished Alcoholic Patients:
Provide an adequate diet and abstention from alcohol.

Nutritional supplements have been used to replace nutrients deficient in malnourished alcoholics in an attempt to improve their overall health.

The Nutritional Cure:
Does NOT exist. Although various nutritional approaches have been touted as "cures" for alcoholism, there is little evidence to support such claims.

The Real World with Dan Knippel, LCSW

When Progress Stalls:
Keeping receipts & examining yearly totals.

PROBLEM:
Sometimes clients are able to reduce their substance use initially but then stop making progress. Maybe they use less than before, but the goal was to quit and they are still using. After initial success and excitement, the client gets stuck.

Here are two techniques a clinician can use to help un-stick the stuck client:
    1) Add up the yearly totals and,
    2) focus on reducing the big yearly total by paying close attention to the weekly totals.

WHAT YOU CAN DO:
Part 1: Add up the yearly totals. (For alcohol, have the client keep receipts for all alcohol purchases for two weeks.) Get out some paper and take an accurate accounting of how much your client is using in a day or week. Then add it all up and give a yearly total. This is usually a very big number and can add perspective that may have been missing.

Example #1: Your client admits to drinking beer every day but said he has cut down since starting sessions with you. Instruct him to keep all alcohol receipts. After two weeks, you add up all the receipts and find he averages $11.00 per day, or $77.00 per week. That means your client, even after cutting down since the start of counseling, still spends more than $4000 per year.

Example #2: Your client admits to drinking about 12 beers per day. That's a total of about 4360 beers per year.

Part 2: Focus on reducing the big yearly total. Instruct your client to keep a journal of when, where, and how much he buys and/or how much he uses each day. Use the yearly totals from Technique #1 as a baseline and see if you and your client can reduce the weekly use enough to make a noticeable difference to the big yearly totals.

Example: Your client has a baseline of drinking about 4360 beers per year. You and he came up with a strategy where he will only buy one 6-pack at a time, instead of his usual 12-pack. During the first week, he bought only one 6-pack each day and only drank three beers one of the days. That is only about 5 beers per day. Wow! Your client reduced his yearly total from 4360 to 1825 in just one week. He just cut down his alcohol use by over 2500 beers per year with one simple change!

Remember to reinforce (also known as *affirming*) desired behavior: "It must feel great to be drinking 2500 less beers per year! Good job."

DESIRED OUTCOME:
Expect your client to be able to relate to the big numbers. He will have a better perspective of how drug and alcohol use can be affecting his health, his finances, and his future. When he can make small changes to his daily behavior that translate into big changes in his yearly totals, he will usually respond well to the praise and encouragement from you to keep chipping away at the totals until he reaches his goal.

Substance Use & Alcohol
www.MyMSW.info

Lesson # 14

COMPLICATIONS – Part 3:

Alcohol abuse and dependence are often associated with physical disorders and related problems including malnutrition.

Malnutrition
Excessive drinking can interfere with the absorption, digestion, metabolism, and utilization of nutrients, particularly vitamins.

Alcoholics will often use alcohol as a source of caloric intake while excluding other food sources, which may account for increase in nutrient deficiency and malnutrition.

Alcoholics in the late stage of the disease often develop anorexia, severe loss of appetite, and a refusal to eat. A significant proportion of patients hospitalized for malnutrition are alcoholics. [Moses 2013].

Alcohol has a direct effect, which can be toxic, on the small bowel including a decrease in absorption of water-soluble vitamins like thiamine, folate, and B6.

Studies have suggested that alcoholism is the most common cause of vitamin and trace element deficiency in the United States among adults.

It is important to know that the effects of Alcohol are dose dependent, which means the more you drink the greater the effect and can result in malnutrition, mal-absorption, and ethanol toxicity [Van den Berg 2002]. The vitamins most involved in wound healing and cell maintenance, A, C, D, E, K, and the B complex series, are deficient in many alcoholics. Lack of vitamin K, which is a part of the blood clotting routine, can cause poor clotting, delayed clotting and can allow excessive bleeding after injury.

Night Blindness is associated with a vitamin A deficiency.

Other vitamin, involved in brain functions, when deficient, can cause severe neurological damage. These deficiencies include folic acid, pyridoxine, thiamine, iron, and zinc).

Wernicke-Korsakoff Syndrome:
A devastating neurological complication, which is evidenced by cerebellar degeneration, dementia, and peripheral neuropathy, can occur from a Thiamine deficiency from chronic heavy alcohol consumption [Thomson 2000].

Thiamine deficiency in alcoholics with Wernicke-Korsakoff syndrome leads to lesions and increased microhemorrhages (small brain bleeds) in the mammillary bodies, thalamus, and brainstem.

Infectious Diseases
Alcohol abuse is a major risk factor for many infectious diseases, especially pulmonary infections [Zhang 2002].

Alcohol Abuse is associated with...

Pneumonia:
Pneumonia is an inflammatory condition of the lung —affecting primarily the microscopic air sacs known as alveoli.

Tuberculosis:
A common, and in many cases lethal, infectious disease caused by various strains of mycobacteria, usually Mycobacterium tuberculosis. Tuberculosis typically attacks the lungs, but can also affect other parts of the body. It is spread through the air when people who have an active TB infection cough, sneeze, or otherwise transmit respiratory fluids.

Among alcohol dependent individuals, other infectious diseases which are that are over-represented are:

Bacterial Meningitis:
An infection, caused by bacteria, in the sac surrounding the brain and spinal cord.

Peritonitis:
An inflammation of the peritoneum, the thin tissue that lines the inner wall of the abdomen and covers most of the abdominal organs.

Less Serious Infections Include:
Chronic Sinusitis:
Sinusitis or rhinosinusitis is inflammation of the paranasal sinuses. It can be due to infection, allergy, or autoimmune issues.

Pharyngitis:
Is a sore throat caused by inflammation of the back of the throat? Your throat may be scratchy and swallowing can be painful.

The Real World with Dan Knippel, LCSW

Awareness + Behavior Change = Success.
Once You Identify the Problems,
Guide Your Client to Behavior Change.

PROBLEM:

Awareness by itself does not cause change in behavior. Clients need to go from talking about their problems to physically doing something to change them. For some, just getting started on their goals becomes a struggle in itself.

Helping a client do something new is tricky and can be your biggest challenge. In session, your client might say change is needed, ("I've just got to quit.") and he talks about what to do to get started. Yet, week after week, he shows up to sessions without having done anything.

Some clinicians are very good at raising awareness but stop short of partnering with the client to make the physical changes necessary to be successful. Sometimes, once the treatment plan is done and the goals and objectives are written down, the clinician stops working and expects the client to simply do the things on the plan. However, the treatment plan does not work itself and your client has proven he has a history of difficulty doing these tasks on his own. He's in counseling with you, after all. You are still very much in this game long after the treatment plan is done.

Initially, you use your sessions to raise awareness of the problems and potential solutions. Some ways to raise awareness include the Spinner Activity, the Good and Not as Good Activity, creating a calendar, demonstrating the "chain" of substance use behaviors, and making lists of supportive people and pro-social activities.

You find out what motivates the client to change, you listen for and elicit change talk; you summarize everything the client says he wants to do. Soon enough, though, it becomes time to stop talking and start doing.

WHAT YOU CAN DO:
Use your session time to complete some small (or large) part of his tasks.

Example: If your client has too much free time and said that volunteering at the local animal shelter is something he wants to do, then use your session time to have him call the animal shelter and make an appointment.

If he wants to walk one hour a day –
  use 5 minutes of each session to walk. Start somewhere.
If he wants to get up earlier and exercise –
  change your session times to the earliest available.
If he wants to transfer control of his money to his wife –
  fill out the direct deposit forms in session.
If he wants to go to NA meetings –
  schedule your sessions an hour after the NA meeting.
If he wants to start a bank account –
  use your office computer to find a no-fee savings account.
If he still hasn't started a bank account –
  seal his $5 bill in an envelope and mark it "Bank Account".
If he still hasn't started a bank account –
  meet him at the bank and talk outside briefly, then complete the session once he has opened the account.

Each of the above examples is an approximation of the ultimate goal. Most importantly, it is an opportunity for the client to convince himself that he can do something new. Now that the client has accomplished a small part of his goal and received some reinforcement from you, he is more likely to do the next small part until he has made real, tangible change. Substance abusers are often prisoners of self-destructive habits developed over the course of years. Expect your client to need a little time and help to learn new, positive habits.

Behavior changes need to be simple and achievable. If your client is struggling with starting his behavior changes, you can help him by setting up easy initial tasks and providing praise and reinforcement.

DESIRED OUTCOME:
Expect your client to either,
- a) complete the initial tasks with your help and encouragement and respond well to the verbal reinforcement, or,
- b) persistently fail to complete even the easiest tasks.

If the client continues to fail to begin their behavior change goals, it is time to reassess the client's readiness to change.

Substance Use & Alcohol
www.MyMSW.info

Lesson # 15

COMPLICATIONS – Part 5:

Cancer
Heavy drinking increases the risk of cancer of the upper gastrointestinal and respiratory tracts

Almost 50 percent of cancers of the mouth, pharynx, and larynx and approximately 75 percent of esophageal cancers in the U.S. are associated with chronic, excessive alcohol consumption [Stinson 1992].

Alcohol consumption and tobacco use increase the risk of esophageal cancer by as much as 130-fold in one study.
[Zambon 2000].

Alcohol consumption increases the risk of breast cancer in women who drink by increasing the production of estradiol.

ALCOHOL/ACETAMINOPHEN INTERACTION
Enzyme CYP2E1:
Chronic heavy drinking appears to activate the enzyme CYP2E1, which may be responsible for transforming the over-the-counter pain reliever acetaminophen into toxic metabolites that can cause liver damage.

Even when acetaminophen is taken in standard therapeutic doses, liver damage has been reported [Girre 1993].

A review of studies of liver damage resulting from acetaminophen-alcohol interaction reported that, in alcoholics, these effects may occur with as little as 2.6 grams of acetaminophen (4 to 5 "extra-strength" pills) taken over the course of the day by persons consuming varying amounts of alcohol [Black 1984].

The Damage:
Damage caused by alcohol-acetaminophen interaction is more likely to occur when acetaminophen is taken after, rather than before, the alcohol has been metabolized.

Moderate drinkers should also be made aware of this potential for interaction. There is now a warning label on the bottle that states: "If you consume three or more alcoholic drinks every day, ask your doctor whether you should take acetaminophen or other pain relievers/ fever reducers."

The Real World with Dan Knippel, LCSW

Excessive Free Time: The Enemy of Abstinence. Part 2, The Spinner Activity.
Demonstrating the Need for More Activities

PROBLEM:
It seems like many drug and alcohol users have a hard time coming up with new, sober activities to fill their ample free time. (See, Excessive Free Time: The Enemy of Abstinence. Part 1.) The resulting boredom becomes a potent trigger to use.

WHAT YOU CAN DO:
Try using a spinner from a board game to illustrate the need for new activities and obligations. Here is your scenario:

Your client is a 55-year-old male you have worked with for three weeks. He has a pattern of frequent relapses. He said, "When I am bored I go get high. Normal people just go to work or volunteer or something, but I just sit at home and watch TV." He said his goal is to stop using drugs and to learn new ways to be active. Unfortunately, he has been very slow to try new coping techniques or to do something with his time even though you and he discuss it in sessions.

Use the spinner from the Milton Bradley® game Twister®, or something similar. You could even make your own. Your client said, "I smoke pot when I'm bored." Therefore, you will label all the choices on the spinner with the word "POT".

Now, have him spin the spinner and it will land on drug use 100% of the time until he adds new strategies for dealing with boredom. The fun part is adding new, safe, and sober choices. When the client incorporates a new strategy, change one of the choices on the spinner.

Ultimately, the client should only have sober choices on the spinner board.

The options for success are limitless. Healthy, safe choices for coping with boredom include:

bike riding	walking
reading	AA or NA
painting	puzzles
volunteering	a job
joining clubs	model building
gardening	collecting
meditation	cooking
take a class	learn a language
clean something	go to the movies

DESIRED OUTCOME:
Your client has already admitted that he has too much free time. Now, with the aid of the Spinner Activity, he will be able to more easily visualize the need to fill the excessive free time with new, sober activities. Have the client make a list of interests and options, and then get started making them a reality.

Hey, counselor. Don't just talk in a soft voice and nod all the time. Have some fun. This Spinner Activity is just a unique way to use evidence-based treatment (identifying triggers). Make something up.

Substance Use & Alcohol
www.MyMSW.info

Lesson # 16

COMPLICATIONS – Part 5:

Sleep Disorders
Although some people believe that alcohol helps them sleep, chronic excessive drinking can induce sleep disorders by disrupting the sequence and duration of sleep states and by altering total sleep time, as well as the time required to fall asleep [Vitiello 1997]. Specifically, drinking within an hour of bedtime appears to disrupt the second half of the sleep period. The person may sleep poorly during the second half of sleep, awakening from dreams and returning to sleep with difficulty, resulting in daytime fatigue and sleepiness [Vitiello 1997].

Individuals who are alcohol dependent may be at increased risk for sleep apnea, a disorder in which the upper air passage narrows or closes during sleep. The combination of alcohol, obstructive sleep apnea, and snoring increases a person's risk for heart attack, arrhythmia, stroke, and sudden death.

Nervous System Dysfunction
The most common neurologic abnormality among alcohol dependent patients is dementia syndrome, which manifests primarily as impairment in recent memory, and more subtle fluctuations in abstractions, calculations, and other aspects of cognitive functions.

As previously stated, one specific neurological complication resulting from thiamine deficiency is Wernicke-Korsakoff syndrome, which involves delirium, clouded sensorium, confusion, ophthalmoplegia, nystagmus, and ataxia.

Immediate administration of thiamine is usually successful in treating the symptoms, but in some cases permanent memory loss occurs. Once delirium and confusion resolve, there is sometimes a profound loss in recent memory (out of proportion to the other cognitive deficits) and alcoholic peripheral neuropathy, which results in diminished sensitivity to touch, pinprick, and vibration (objectively, and para subjectively).

The acute effects of alcohol on the nervous system are signs people commonly think of when they envision an intoxicated person, such as slurred speech, loss of coordination, unsteady gait, impairment of attention or memory, nystagmus, stupor, or coma. The degree to which the central nervous system is impaired is directly proportional to the BAC.

Alcohol and the Brain
Alcohol affects most neurochemical systems including N-methyl-D aspartate (NMDA), gamma-aminobutyric acid (GABA), serotonin, dopamine (DA), and opioid systems.

Alcohol inhibits NMDA systems, which may contribute to feeling intoxicated. NMDA receptors change as tolerance develops. These receptor systems are overactive during withdrawal. Alcohol also enhances the action of the GABA system, producing some of the symptoms of acute intoxication. GABA receptors are especially sensitive to alcohol. The GABA system is underactive during withdrawal, and the genes that control these receptors may have an impact on the risk of alcohol dependence [Schuckit 1999].

Alcohol causes the release of 5-HT, or serotonin. Lower 5-HT levels in the brain are associated with increased alcohol intake in animals and humans, while higher 5-HT levels are associated with slightly reduced alcohol intake. Several 5-HT genes may be related to the genetic risk of alcohol dependence [Schuckit 2002].

Alcohol activates DA in the reward system in the ventral tegmental area of the brain. Alcohol also causes the release of DA. Several DA receptors may be related to the genetic risk of alcohol dependence [Schuckit 2002].

Finally, alcohol causes the release of endogenous opioids. Opioid receptors change with tolerance and withdrawal. Some receptors may affect genetic predisposition for alcohol dependence and opioid antagonists can decrease voluntary alcohol consumption. Alcohol may also affect acetylcholine, norepinephrine and steroids.

Most people who drink do not develop brain damage. However, studies do indicate that impaired cognition and motor abilities occur in some individuals who are heavy drinkers. Older persons with alcohol dependence exhibit more brain tissue loss than both older and younger persons without alcohol dependence. These results suggest that aging may render a person more susceptible to the effects of chronic excessive alcohol. Most studies suggest that, following long-term abstinence, most brain changes resolve.

Magnetic resonance imaging has been used to measure changes in the brain structure and volume in alcoholics at three weeks after abstinence from alcohol. The results indicated that the brain volume in alcohol dependent men and women was significantly reduced as compared to nonalcoholic dependent men and women. The differences, however, were much more significant in women than in men. These results indicate that alcohol inflicts greater neurotoxic effects in alcohol dependent women than alcohol dependent men, but again, these brain changes may resolve with long-term abstinence.

The Real World with Dan Knippel, LCSW

What if a client wants to stop treatment too soon?

PROBLEM:
Sometimes, clients meet a good therapist (you) and they feel pretty good about themselves after just a few sessions. Clients might leave after two or three sessions instead of participating to the end. They feel good about things today, so they believe they will have the "willpower" to stay clean on their own.

WHAT YOU CAN DO:
First, talk about it early on. During the first session, inform your client that it is normal to want to stop counseling when he gains a little confidence. You might say,

> *"Sometimes people feel a lot better about their situation after just a couple sessions. They believe that, because they feel good today, they don't need to keep coming to counseling. What are your thoughts on that?"*

Second, use good *informed consent* in the first couple sessions to clearly establish the number of recommended counseling sessions. Be clear. Tell your client,

> *"We are going to do at least 12 sessions over the next four months. We will try for one session a week. Our plan is to be as close to your treatment goal as possible by the 12th session."*

Third, try counting backwards.

> *"We're doing 12 sessions to work on your goal and get you where you want to be. We are counting down toward your goal, so this first session is actually #12. We will check one off each*

week as you get closer to your goal, 12, 11, 10, 9, and so on, all the way down to the finish."

Other ideas:
Try physical reminders. Give a token or poker chip for each session. Prepare a paper with 12 spaces, one for each session, and write a little summary in the space each week and some kind of encouragement.

If possible, enlist the help of the client's family or friends to make sure he comes to sessions.

Finally, try a reminder phone call a day in advance.

DESIRED OUTCOME:
Your client will remain engaged in treatment for all the sessions. He will be focused on sobriety longer. You will be a more effective counselor. There will be one less person struggling with chemical dependency. Good job.

Substance Use & Alcohol
www.MyMSW.info

Lesson # 17

Alcohol and its problems:

Alcoholics generally have alcohol problems in conjunction with other medical illnesses and mental health disorders. Lapham (2001) reported that about one-half of women and one-third of men who have a history of alcohol abuse or dependence would be diagnosed with at least one other mental health disorder.

One of the more difficult aspects of alcohol abuse is that alcohol can function as both a stimulant and as a depressant, depending on when the drinking occurs and the quantity of alcohol used. According to Regier (1990) one-third to one-half of alcoholics also are afflicted with a Major Depressive Disorder during their abuse. It is important to understand that more than three-quarters of men and women who are identified as alcoholics will also meet the criteria for a Major Depressive Disorder (Regier 1990). The reason we need to be aware of depression as a comorbid condition with alcoholism is simple. If depression is untreated, sometime during the treatment the alcoholic will leave treatment and relapse.

One of the reasons alcoholics are often diagnosed as depressed is due to the similarity of symptoms between alcohol abuse and depression. There is a mimicry that can be hard to sort out during the diagnostic phase.

The fact that 'binge drinking" and severe alcohol intoxication can also cause mood swings, and the "manic-like" behaviors we associate with Bipolar disorder, does not make the diagnosis any easier. During the course of the disease, we will also notice insomnia, decreased appetite, temporary depressive symptoms and a general decrease in overall energy, even if the abuser has no history of a depressive illness.

Other things to look for include cirrhosis (swelling) of the liver, anti-social and other personality disorders, nicotine dependence, hepatitis, eating disorders, anxiety disorders, major depressive disorder and, of course, bipolar disorder.

Currently, we do not know by what mechanism depression and alcohol dependence are intertwined; however, both conditions share very similar risk factors. It is absolutely important to treat the Co-Morbid disorders your client arrives with, in order to prevent serious adverse consequences much as suicide.

Because alcohol often makes depression worse, it can be a significant factor in suicide. Therefore, identifying the risk factors associated with alcohol abuse and dependence are absolutely essential.

According to the American Association of Suicidality (AAS), Suicide is the 11th leading cause of death overall and the 3rd leading cause among persons 15 to 34 years of age. According to the AAS, in 2007, 34,598 people in the United States committed suicide and an estimated 864,950 attempted suicide.

Cornelius (1996) found that as many as 85 percent of individuals who commit suicide suffer from depression or alcohol dependence, and 70 percent of alcoholics with comorbid depression report that they have made a suicide attempt at some point in their lives. Alcohol abuse and dependence can exaggerate depression and increase the chance of an impulsive act including aggression, suicide, and violent ideations.

In the alcohol dependent population, fifteen to twenty people out of a hundred will attempt suicide. Of those who have attempted suicide in the past, fifteen to twenty people out of a hundred will attempt a second time within five years of the first attempt.

Alcoholism and Suicide:
Effective prevention of suicide and suicidal behaviors can only be achieved if the providers are competent and skilled at obtaining both a substance abuse history and a psychiatric history. Experience has shown that with abstinence from alcohol for fourteen to twenty-one days and good nutrition, the depressive effects of alcohol begin to recede. Alcohol and drug dependence are second only to age in determining the most important risk factors in a Suicide Risk Assessment. If you look at

the populations who have attempted suicide, nine out of ten will have a diagnosable mental health disorder according to Mann (2002).

Among the population that will attempt suicide, alcohol dependence is common. Alcohol is the number one drug of abuse associated with suicide. The most commonly diagnosed mental health disorders in mental health patients are Major Depressive Disorder and Alcohol Dependence. This information allows us to target our resources quickly when determining patient triage.

Often, alcohol is involved in suicide attempts by "driving a vehicle" and suicide by "overdose." Some of the reason we believe this connection exists comes from alcohol's ability to impair judgment, block physical pain and lower the survival threshold.

Preuss (2002) has estimated the overall suicide risk for an alcohol dependent individual was about one in ten, which is five to ten times higher than seen in the general population. Murphy (1990) has placed the likelihood of suicide for those diagnosed with Alcohol Dependence as sixty to one hundred twenty times higher than individuals without alcohol involvement.

The Real World with Dan Knippel, LCSW

Avoid asking "Why?"
It feels like an interrogation and often may not promote change.

PROBLEM:
Why do therapists ask "Why?"? Therapists may have been taught in school to ask "Why?" a client does something. Maybe the therapist has a personal belief that asking "Why?" a client did something will lead to a "break through" or some amazing awareness.

> "Why did you relapse again? You said you were going to quit".
> "Why are you spending so much money on drugs? Your family needs that money."
> "You're still drinking. Why aren't you using the tools we talked about?"
> *(See below for alternatives to these "Why?" questions.)*

The above "Why?" questions are inappropriate if your goal is to help motivate a client to change. Unfortunately, some therapists still use language like this in counseling. Asking "Why?" implies that you lack understanding of the client's problem. Furthermore, asking "Why?" might give him the feeling he is being scolded or reprimanded.

Clinicians use their education and knowledge to guide their practice. Sometimes, asking "Why?" can make a therapist appear less qualified. If you can reasonably answer the question yourself, don't ask.

Moreover, asking "Why?" is *problem-focused*. Focusing on the client's strengths and goals may be a better use of therapy time.

WHAT YOU CAN DO:
Resist the temptation to ask "Why?". The solution to substance abuse problems often comes from a focus on the future, toward what new skills need to be learned and used.

Alternatives to the "Why?" questions above include,
> "You had another relapse. Where do you go from here?"
> "We can talk about what it felt like to spend so much money in one night, or we could talk about strategies to avoid heavy spending in the future."
> "There are some of the things getting in the way of your abstinence goal."

DESIRED OUTCOME:
Your client will focus on his sobriety goals and not question your knowledge or be focused on his failures. You want to guide the client toward the change he wants.

NOTE: Avoiding asking "Why?" is a huge topic and has applications in many areas of clinical counseling. This topic was inspired by:
> Brodsky, S.L. (2011). Therapy With Coerced and Reluctant Clients. American Psychological Association; Washington, D.C.

Substance Use & Alcohol
www.MyMSW.info

Lesson # 18

Brief Interventions

Approximately 20 percent of patients seeking treatment in Primary Care have drinking behaviors, which put them at serious risk for developing alcohol dependency and other problems.

Alcohol abuse has very serious consequences. In the short-term it can cause family, social and occupational issues. In the long-term it can cause disease, damage and death. Mental health professionals are not always very good at identifying and responding to alcohol and drug abuse.

Even mental health professionals who can identify alcohol and substance abuse quickly may not be able to provide adequate treatment due to knowledge and skill deficits or socio-economic barriers.

Even if the mental health professional knows what to do, the patient's refusal to accept help can often cause the problems for the treating professionals.

Once immediate safety has been achieved and there is no need for or ability to access long-term treatment, brief intervention can help to reduce the risk of the disease. It generally takes the form of one, two or three sessions lasting from fifteen minutes to two hours.

The format of the intervention will vary with the severity of the problem. Patients who have already achieved alcohol dependence will need more intervention than those who are at a less serious stage of the disease. These patients may need only a very brief intervention.

The goals for the alcohol dependent patient may be much more complicated, like total abstinence or referral to a comprehensive treatment program, while the goals for the less serious patient may entail simpler interventions, including harm-reduction through reduced drinking.

The FRAMES approach to Brief Intervention

The acronym FRAMES refers to six different aspects of an intervention. These aspects are:
- Feedback of Personal Risk
- Responsibility
- Advice
- Menu of strategies
- Empathy
- Self-efficacy

Feedback of Personal Risk

The mental health provider uses the patient's current drinking behaviors, any lab tests and any actual or potential consequences of the behavior to provide direct feedback about the risk of alcohol becoming a problem, or the extent to which alcohol is a problem.

Responsibility of the Patient:

The mental health provider encourages the patient to recognize their own responsibility and their choice to continue or change the drinking behavior. This intervention gives the patient a sense of personal control in the change process at a time when they may feel very "out of control."

Advice to Change:

The mental health provider gives the patient recommendations and information about moderating drinking and the reduction of risk that can be achieved by reducing or stopping their drinking behavior.

Menu of Ways to Reduce Drinking:

The mental health provider provides information on strategies and tactics on cutting back on or avoiding alcohol consumption. These include setting limits, recognizing reason for drinking, and how to gain skills to avoid high risk drinking. This may include giving documentation like "drinking diaries" to help them monitor their behavior.

Empathetic Counseling Style:
Confrontational methods are not very effective when trying to gain patient trust. Generally the alcohol dependent patient will have very confrontational treatment in the past and will have developed skills to blunt their effectiveness.

Self-Efficacy or Optimism of the Patient:
Encourage and support the patient in creating a plan to change their behavior, which would include skills to allow them to develop positive cognitions around their ability to stop drinking.

Other important interventions include:

Establishing a Drinking Goal:
All patients should be encouraged and supported in establishing a drinking goal during the intervention. Often, this drinking goal should be in writing. The drinking goal can range from drinking reduction to complete abstinence.

& Follow-up:
Very Important! Follow-up phone calls, letters or repeat visits to the patient will help the development of a therapeutic bond.

Behavior change is more likely when the patient recognizes they have a problem and are ready, willing and able to embrace a goal. They become more optimistic about their chances of success. It is important to constantly monitor their readiness to change.

Just because a patient is not currently ready for change does not mean they will not be ready at their next visit, or their next crisis. You, as the mental health provider, should always be ready to assist the patient the moment they contact the system.

Change is slow.

You may embark on change many times without success. The chance of "falling off the wagon" is always very high and should not be a deterrent to your intervention. In fact, you should anticipate repeated failure. Your initial progress may simply be an increased amount of time between alcohol-induced crises.

A patient, who is admitted weekly for stabilization, for months on end, and transitions to one admit every month, is a success story.

The road away from alcohol dependence is long, winding and fraught with bars at every intersection. Be patient. Be Supportive.

The Real World
with
Dan Knippel, LCSW

What if your client needs residential treatment but has no way of paying for it? Look for faith-based programs!

PROBLEM:
Sometimes, a client's struggles with sobriety are too difficult to change without getting away from his environment. He may be unable to avoid "unsafe" people or places. Whatever the reason, sometimes residential treatment is necessary. Unfortunately, for many adults without insurance, residential treatment is out of reach. However, faith-based residential programs offer an excellent alternative. Many programs are run by small missions or church groups and provide an option for adults who cannot pay for private residential care.

WHAT YOU CAN DO:
Link your client with faith-based residential programs. Faith-based programs often have short wait lists, charge little or no money, and clients can stay longer than most private programs.

Most faith-based programs require the client to pay some small portion of their monthly income (if they have any) and/or the client will usually work at the program's Thrift Store or other fund-raising enterprise. For example, Teen Challenge is a faith-based program where clients can be seen working for the program's car washing business. Other programs may have lawn maintenance or painting businesses to help with expenses, so your client needs to be able to work.

Faith-based programs exist around the country but can be difficult to find. Do not expect to find faith-based programs with an Internet search alone. It is also important to know that there may only be one or two in your state.

The best way to find faith-based programs is to ask other substance abuse counselors. Locate a few substance abuse treatment programs in neighboring cities, then call and ask those counselors about the faith-based programs they know about.

Keep in mind that faith-based programs are just that: faith-based. The main treatment models will likely be based on religion and 12-Steps.

DESIRED OUTCOME: Your client will have access to residential treatment. Faith-based programs are especially useful for adult males without insurance and adult females without children or insurance.

Substance Use & Alcohol
www.MyMSW.info

Lesson # 19

Substance Abuse treatment is effective!

Patients who decide to stop drinking can find the treatment and support needed to quit, remain sober, and regain their lives. Like all treatments, having a full understanding of the options is important to making good, informed choices.

PHASES OF TREATMENT

There are FOUR PHASES to treatment.

Assessment and Evaluation:
Of symptoms life problems, treatment choices and plan development.

Detoxification:
Stopping use

Active treatment:
Consists of any and all of the following – Residential programs, therapeutic communities, intensive and regular outpatient treatment, medications for alcohol craving reduction, medications to discourage alcohol use, medications to treat co-morbid mental health issues, 12-step programs, other self-help/mutual-help groups.

Maintaining sobriety and relapse prevention:
Ongoing outpatient treatment, 12-step programs, other self-help/mutual-help groups.

Assessment and Evaluation:
Step one is for the Alcoholic to overcome denial and distorted thinking. This is followed by the desire to begin treatment. At this point, the alcohol dependent individual must get help from someone knowledgeable and competent in the treatment of this disorder.

At this stage in the illness, some individuals have lost most control over their alcohol use. They may be able to make immediate decisions only. The most basic goal is to quit drinking. You may be able to develop a detailed plan but you may also need to wait until the patient is post-detoxification.

The issues encountered with this stage center around DENIAL. This denial may be almost universal, or the individual may show some level of insight into their problem.

Your treatment plan should be developed based on the level of insight and the amount of the denial an individual exhibits. This is the point where a trained addiction specialist is absolutely necessary to assist the patient.

Detoxification
This phase of treatment involves quitting use. Sometimes called "Cold Turkey." It can be done on an inpatient setting or in an outpatient setting. Regardless of the setting, medical evaluation and treatment are very important at this stage. Many alcohol dependent individuals will develop dangerous withdrawal symptoms that need medical management in a hospital or in an outpatient setting. Simply removing the alcohol does not automatically produce positive, complete outcomes.

Medical Management of Withdrawal Symptoms:
Abrupt cessation of drinking, as well as simply "cutting back" may produce a number of specific withdrawal symptoms when an individual is physically dependent. These symptoms include:

Sweating	Rapid heartbeat
Hypertension	Tremors
Anorexia	Insomnia
Agitation	Anxiety
Nausea	Vomiting

Delirium Tremens:
Is a central nervous system symptom of alcohol withdrawal that may occur in the first 96 hours of quitting alcohol? It is often seen in chronic alcoholism. Symptoms include:

Uncontrollable trembling	Hallucinations
Severe anxiety	Sweating
Sudden feelings of terror	

The Revised Clinical Institute Withdrawal Assessment for Alcohol Scale (CIWA-Ar) is a symptom-triggered, 10-item scale that quantifies the risk and severity of alcohol withdrawal. This instrument can be found in Appendix A.

Often, withdrawal symptoms are treated with benzodiazepines. This class of drug reduces related anxiety, restlessness, insomnia, tremors, DT, and withdrawal seizures.

However, both short-acting and long- acting benzodiazepines have their problems. The long-acting benzodiazepines can decrease rebound symptoms and work for long periods of time, but intramuscular absorption can be very erratic. Short-acting benzodiazepines have less risk of over sedation. Yet, breakthrough symptoms can and do occur, and risk of seizure is imminent.

Patients undergoing withdrawal are generally treated with diazepam or chlordiazepoxide. If intramuscular administration is necessary, Lorazepam is the drug of choice.

Anticonvulsants are also used for safe withdrawal. They cannot be abused and there is almost no risk of seizures. They do not help with the symptoms of delirium and they can have some liver toxicity. Detoxification is only one of many steps in the treatment process, and the beginning of a lifelong process.

Active Treatment
The first decision for active treatment is acute hospitalization vs. inpatient detoxification. While hospitalization can be cost-effective, it is not always available...

Inpatient hospitalization is indicated for the following:
    acute withdrawal symptoms
    failed outpatient detoxification

      appears depressed
      unstable home situation
      possibility of family disruption or job loss

If in doubt, call a physician who specialized in alcohol treatment to error on the side of caution and attempt to secure inpatient hospitalization. This first three to six months is a period characterized by mood changes, anxiety, depression, insomnia, physiological changes and sleep problems.

This time frame is critical for sobriety. Active support is constantly necessary.

The second phase of active treatment can last for 6 months to many years. Here is where the patient gains the motivation and skills to stay sober. They are in the process of building the support systems they need in order to cope with the daily issues they avoided through their alcohol use.

During this phase, a treatment professional is very important. A professional can help them understand how alcohol has affected their life and can help them develop goals and plans to maintain sobriety.

Some proven medications are available to help with alcohol craving and to discourage alcohol use and will be discussed in detail later in this course.

This **stage** is where some medications and treatments are most effective. It is also the stage where other medications can be used to treat co-morbid psychiatric conditions including depression and anxiety.

All of our research indicates the longer a patient maintains sobriety, the longer they stay in treatment, the more active and involved their commitment is, the greater the chance to remain sober.

This is a time when support groups, especially AA can help achieve and maintain sobriety.

Maintaining Sobriety and Relapse Prevention

The dividing line between active treatment and the maintenance phase of recovery is very blurry. Sometimes it is almost impossible to establish.

During the active phase, the patient learns what is needed to stay sober and they develop skills to avoid relapsing. During the maintenance phase the person is using the skills learned to handle the curve balls life throws at them. Many patients attribute their ongoing sobriety to support group participation. These groups range from AA to NA to Women for Sobriety.

The Real World with Dan Knippel, LCSW

Clients often blame the treatment program for failing them, saying, "it" did not work. Help the client realize they are "it".

PROBLEM:
Sometimes, clients participate in many different treatment programs over their lifetime. Clients with recurring abuse or dependence problems often say, "I went to that program, but it didn't work", or, "I tried AA, but it didn't change anything", or, "That inpatient program was a waste of time, it didn't teach me anything."
The client is blaming the program for his own failure and past lack of motivation.

WHAT YOU CAN DO:
Explore the possibility that the client is "it". He is coping with his failure by redirecting the blame onto the program. Try humor and sarcasm if you have appropriate rapport:

"I bought a gym membership, but it didn't work."

Maybe try something similar in spirit to Motivational Enhancement Therapy's "amplified reflection". Try these on your client:

"Sure, you don't see how anybody could benefit from one of those programs."

Try to focus on the solution with an open-ended question like:

"Pretend you went to a program that worked. What would it be like in that program that made it work?"

The idea is to help the client come to understand that programs don't "work"; clients make them work for themselves. Every program works for somebody.

DESIRED OUTCOME: Your client will have a better awareness that they are "it". Your guidance will help the client discover that he is what "works".

In response to your sarcasm, the client may "catch himself" and say, "OK, I get it. If I want it to work I have to work it."

He should try to correct your amplified reflection by saying something like, "Well, no, a lot of guys got sober in the program, it just wasn't right for me at the time."

Your solution-focused question may help him define what he feels would help him most.

Substance Use & Alcohol

Lesson # 20

**Alcoholics Anonymous
And Other 12-Step Programs**

The grandfather of alcohol treatment is Alcoholics Anonymous. AA is a self-help organization founded in 1935. AA changed the way professionals thought about alcohol dependence and treatment. AA developed a successful 12-step program by combining self-help with a spiritual foundation. It then firmly planted itself in the fellowship of recovering alcoholics.

You do not need to be religious to be in AA.

AA is run solely by recovering alcoholics and is in almost every community with specific programs, meeting and locations. If you need to find a meeting go to www.aa.org. It also provides round the clock assistance.

There are no membership dues and it is open to everyone.

AA promotes and provides fellowship. This fellowship can be very positive and can help counterbalance feelings of grief, loss, and shame associated with alcohol dependence.

AA and other 12-step programs provide effective treatment programs that facilitate long-term abstinence after treatment.

AA also provides an important group process therapy for dependent alcoholics.

AA prescribes keeping it simple, taking it one day at a time, and avoiding the people, places, and things associated with their use. This approach is a powerful tool for relapse prevention.

AA also helps recovering alcoholics to develop positive lifestyles and find new ways to solve old problems. The feeling of fellowship, support, and guidance helps make getting sober and staying sober more likely.

The reduction of shame and guilt fostered by AA along with its message of the acceptance of powerlessness over drinking is often reported by alcoholics after attending meetings every day.

One of AA's principles is the value of performing services that will help other alcoholics.
Prevention of relapse is an active daily process.

Counseling
Cognitive-behavioral therapies (CBTs) are the most frequently used treatments for substance use disorders.
CBTs have been shown to be effective in several clinical trials of substance users.

Characteristics of CBTs include:
- Social learning and behavioral theories of drug abuse

- An approach summarized as "recognize, avoid, and cope"

- Organization built around a functional analysis of substance use
(for example: understanding the antecedents and consequences of substance use)

- Skill training uses strategies for:
    coping with cravings
    fostering motivation to change
    managing thoughts about drugs
    developing problem-solving skills
    planning for/managing high-risk situations
    cultivating drug refusal skills

Basic principles of CBTs include:
- Basic skills should be mastered before more complex ones are given.
- Material presented by the therapist should be matched to patient needs.

- Repetition fosters the development of skills.
- Practice is needed for mastery of skills.
- The patient is an active participant in treatment.
- Skills taught are general enough to be applied to a variety of problem areas.

Structured behavior therapy techniques can be effective components of alcohol dependence treatment. Behavioral therapy techniques are often used in conjunction with CBT's. The goal of a CBT is to increase the patient's engagement in positive activities and socially reinforcing behaviors.

CBT data confirms that:
> Drug abuse patients need motivation and skills to succeed in stopping drug use.
> Research has shown that offering contingent incentives for abstinence can reduce drug abuse behavior.
> The most striking successes have come from positive reinforcement programs that provide contingent incentives for abstinence using money-based vouchers as rewards.
> Research provides examples, but treatment providers may need to be creative in discovering reinforcers that can be used for contingency management in their own clinical settings.

Medications Used to Treat Alcohol Dependence
Some medications are used for detoxification and others are used for relapse prevention. Research has shown that medications must be used in conjunction with talk and other therapies to be most.

Antabuse
Also known as Disulfiram. The FDA approved it for treatment of alcohol dependence in 1951. It works by blocking an enzyme, aldehyde dehydrogenase, the body uses to metabolize alcohol. Drinking while on Disulfiram causes the alcohol at the acetaldehyde stage to accumulate in the blood. This then produces nausea, vomiting, sweating, and even difficulty breathing. Disulfiram is not recommended for patients with diabetes, cardiovascular or cerebrovascular disease, or kidney or liver failure. With the advent of more modern and improved medicines, Disulfiram is often used as a last resort.

Naltrexone
Also called ReVia is an opioid antagonist that interferes with the rewarding or pleasurable effects of alcohol. This allows it to reduce the alcohol craving.

The FDA approved the use of Naltrexone in alcohol dependence in December 1994.

Naltrexone has been proven to:
    Reduce alcohol relapses
    Decrease the possibility of a slip becoming a relapse
    Decrease the total amount of drinking.

The most common side effects are light- headedness, diarrhea, dizziness, and nausea. Side effects tend to disappear quickly. It is not recommended for patients with:
    acute hepatitis
    liver failure
    for adolescents
    pregnant or breastfeeding women

Naltrexone works best integrated into a complete treatment program including traditional 12-step fellowship-based treatments and /or CBT.

Nalmefene
Also called Revex is newer opioid antagonist. It is administered intravenously. It shows no liver toxicity, however method of administration makes its use limited in outpatient settings.

Acamprosate
Also known as Campral is a synthetic compound with a chemical structure similar to naturally occurring amino acid neurotransmitters e.g. homotaurine and GABA. The FDA approved it in July 2004 for the maintenance of alcohol abstinence. It has been used successfully in Europe and around the world for years.

Baclofen
Baclofen is a GABA agonist. In a study of alcohol-dependent patients with liver cirrhosis, baclofen was also found to work favorably in maintenance of alcohol abstinence. Seventy-one percent of baclofen-treated patients maintained abstinence as compared with twenty-nine percent of the placebo group [208].

Anticonvulsants
Topiramate is effective in reducing heavy drinking in alcohol dependent patients. Side effects of Topiramate include numbness in the extremities, fatigue, confusion, paresthesias, depression, change in taste, and weight loss.

Carbamazepine has proven effective for treating acute alcohol withdrawal. Side effects include nausea, vomiting, drowsiness, dizziness, chest pain, headache, trouble urinating, numbness in extremities, liver damage, and allergic reaction.

Oxcarbazepine is a carbamazepine derivative, with fewer side effects than Carbamazepine.

Buspirone Hydrochloride
Also called Buspar, a dopamine antagonist and partial agonist for serotonin, exhibiting anxiolytic properties.

Clozapine
Also called Clozaril is an atypical antipsychotic approved to treat schizophrenia and its resultant symptoms (e.g., hallucinations, suicidal behavior). It has shown promise in the treatment of comorbid substance use.

The Real World with Dan Knippel, LCSW

Do past substance abusers make better substance abuse counselors? What if I was an abstainer?

PROBLEM: Some clinicians worry they will not be effective substance abuse counselors if they do not have experience with substance abuse or dependence themselves. Alternatively, some ex-substance abusers believe that they will be good counselors because of their experience. Neither is true.

WHAT YOU CAN DO:

With a personal history of substance abuse:
- A potential for improved complex reflections and reframing of substance abuse experiences.
- Shared experience may provide comfort in a group setting. (However, change is unlikely to occur just because someone else went through what you did).
- May be less judgmental. May be more judgmental of certain types of users.
- May be able to spot lies or minimizing sooner than a non-user.
- May have a more intimate understanding of trigger mechanisms but may avoid talking about issues that are personal triggers.
- May have more credibility to confront others.
- There is a potential to try to convince a client that the way they got clean will work for them, instead of letting the client choose what feels right. For example, some counselors may push 12-Step programs as "the only way" a person can change.

Without a personal history of substance abuse:
- You do not have to discuss your personal history and you will rarely be asked. Less is better.
- In a group: "I'm not here to teach anyone how to use, I think everyone has that covered already. Instead, we're working together toward the future to get to where you want to be."

- "I'd rather not discuss my history. It's risky because sometimes people would say I'm too much of a lightweight and others might judge me more harshly. Everybody's different."
- Use a complex reflection to direct the focus away from your history: "You want to know there are people who have shared your experience and have gotten through it."
- Use humor: "Man, the last person I told my history to got up and ran. How would you feel if we just stuck with looking forward from today?"
- *You do not have to have a broken leg to fix one or to know it hurts. You don't have to drive a hatchback to help someone change a tire on one. Be yourself.*

DESIRED OUTCOME: Substance abuse counseling is the same as any other profession; it takes training and practice to gain the necessary skills to be effective.

You do not have to experience alcoholism or drug addiction to empathize and provide quality, professional clinical care. Additionally, clients may appreciate when you keep your sobriety ideology to yourself.

Substance Use & Alcohol
www.MyMSW.info

Lesson # 21

Motivational Interviewing Defined...

MI is an evidence-based clinical practice used in the treatment of individuals with substance use disorders.

MI focuses on ambivalence, on exploring and resolving the centers of the motivational processes within the individual in order to facilitate change. It is different from other methods that are viewed as coercive or externally driven as a way of motivating change.

External methods do not appear to have the same success of MI because they impose change that may be inconsistent with the person's values, beliefs or wishes. MI supports a person's change in a manner that runs parallel to that person's values and concerns.

The MI Approach places interviewing in a grounded and respectful stance that focuses on building rapport during the initial stages of the therapeutic relationship.

MI centers on identification, examination, and resolution of ambivalence concerning a person's changing behavior. *Ambivalence*, the feeling of wanting to change and wanting to stay the same, at the same time, is seen as a natural issue in the change process and not an aberration.

Using MI allows the interventionist to "tune in to" the person's ambivalence, therefore allowing the interventionist to recognize ambivalence and "readiness for change." They are then able to use these strategies thoughtfully with the responsive client.

MI includes three essential elements.

> First it is a specific type of conversation about the change a client wants to and needs to embrace.

Second, it is a collaborative effort that places the client at the center and honors the autonomy of the client. It assumes the client is the expert and supports the client in bringing forth their expertise.

Finally, MI seeks to call forth the client's own motivation and commitment. It evokes client change by evoking internal responses. It is internally driven, not externally forced.
To the non-professional MI is a collaborative conversation used to strengthen the client's own motivation to change.

For the professional, MI is a person-centered counseling method which allows the client to address their common, acknowledged issues and their internal ambivalence regarding the need to change.

MI is a collaborative, goal directed method of communication between the interventionist and the client, with a very specific focus on the "language of change." It is designed to strengthen an individual's motivation for and movement toward a specific goal by eliciting and exploring the person's own arguments for change.

MI is more than just a set of technical interventions. It is an intervention set with a spirit. This "spirit", or "way of being" involves the technical aspects of MI as the play out in the context of the client-therapist relationship. One cannot be divorced from the other.

The SPIRIT of MI can be understood if you can visualize the intervention resting on three, very specific elements. They are:

1) Collaboration between the client and therapist
2) Drawing out the client's ideas for change
3) Placing the emphasis for change on the client.

- **Collaboration (vs. Confrontation)**

Collaboration is a partnership formed between the therapist and the client, grounded in the point of view and experiences of the client. This partnership removes the therapist from the "expert role" and keeps the

therapist from imposing their perspective on the client's substance use patterns.
This collaboration allows the building of rapport and allows the client to develop a deep level of trust in the relationship. It keeps the relationship on a more unilateral level, instead of a hierarchical relationship.

It is important to remember this collaboration does not mean the therapist and the client will agree on the problem, its scope or its solution. The MI therapeutic process is focused on mutual understanding.

- **Evocation (Drawing Out, Rather Than Imposing Ideas)**

MI values the therapist's ability to assist the client and "draw out" their ideas, opinions, thoughts and feelings, instead of having the therapist impose their desires, opinions and motivations on the client.

Change due to internal motivation and commitment is more powerful and durable than change related to external motivation. MI purports that lasting change is more likely to occur when the clients discover their own reasons and determination to change. With MI the therapist's job is not to tell them what to do or why they should do it.

- **Autonomy (vs. Authority)**

MI understands that the true power for change rests within the client. Ultimately, it is the individual who needs follow through and make change happen.
This allows empowerment while also allowing the responsibility to rest squarely on the client's shoulders.

In MI, the therapist job is also to help the client understand there is no one "right way" to change, but there are many ways that change can occur.

While clients are encouraged to make changes, they are also encouraged to develop a list or "menu" of various options and how to achieve and implement these options.

In addition to the three pillars of on which rests the "Spirit of MI" there are FOUR distinct principles that guide the practice of MI.

The FOUR Principles of MI

In order to use MI appropriate, you, the therapist must adhere to these principles.

- **Express Empathy**

Empathy requires the therapist see the world through the eyes of the client. This includes thinking about things the way the client thinks and feeling things like the client feels them.

This principle allows for clients to be heard and understood, and in turn, it is more likely the clients will share their experiences honestly. If the client is able to feel the therapist can see their world from their point of view, the process of EMPATHY has been effective.

- **Support Self-Efficacy**

MI is a strength-based approach, based on the idea client have the capacity to change within themselves. They simple need assistance accessing this ability. IN order for change to occur the client must be able to believe in the possibility of change. The therapist role is to help instill the hope necessary for the changes to occur. This belief in an ability to change is called self-efficacy.

This is not always an easy task, as clients have often tried to change in the past and have failed; now doubting their abilities. The MI therapist will always support this self-efficacy through focus on previous success and client skill and strength.

- **Roll with Resistance**

MI therapists believe that resistance to change comes from previous unsuccessful changes and where a client perceives a conflict between their view of the "problem" or "solution" and the clinician's view of the "problem" or "solution". This conflict violates the freedom and autonomy of the client that results in frustration in failure.

The MI therapist will avoid creating or eliciting resistance. Avoiding confrontation does this when resistance occurs. The therapist will de-escalate the situation and avoid a negative interaction. This is known as "rolling with it."

When the client demonstrates actions of makes statements that demonstrate resistance, these should remain unchallenged by the MI therapist during the early stages of the therapeutic relationship.
When the therapist "rolls with the resistance" they disrupts any "struggle" that can occur during the session. This lack of resistance keeps the client from avoiding change by playing the games of "devil's advocate" or "yes, but" when the counselor makes suggestions. MI places a high value on the client's ability to define the problem and to develop his or her own solutions. This approach makes it difficult for the client to resist change.

When exploring the clients concerns, the therapist invites the client to examine a new point of view without presenting the therapists point of view. Finally, the therapist needs to avoid the tendency to make sure the client understands and agrees with the need to change. This is known as the "righting reflex." The MI therapist avoids using this "righting reflex" at all times during a session.

- **Develop Discrepancy**

This occurs when the therapist is able to help the client see the mismatch between "where they are and where they want to be." This awareness creates the motivation to change. The MI therapist helps to client develop this by helping them examine the discrepancies between their current circumstances/behavior and their values and future goals.

Once the client realizes their current behaviors place them in conflict with either their values or goals, they are more likely to increase their motivation to make the changes they need in order to reduce the conflict.

The MI therapist should never use strategies that create conflict and discrepancy. They should help the client slowly become aware of the discrepancy between their behavior and their progress towards their current goals.

createspace

PS:LBX0B4232211

CreateSpace
7290 Investment Drive Suite B
North Charleston, SC 29418

Question About Your Order?

"Log in to your account at www.createspace.com and "Contact Support.""

12/11/2014 10:36:19 AM
Order ID: 77995352

Qty.	Item	

IN THIS SHIPMENT

| 1 | Substance Use & Alcohol | 149537209X |

The Real World with Dan Knippel, LCSW

Measuring treatment success using a simple, custom assessment questionnaire.

PROBLEM:

How do you know your treatment is successful? How do you keep track of whether or not the client feels he is benefitting from the treatment? A good way to measure success and change over time is by using a simple custom assessment questionnaire. It is called "custom" because the assessment questions are custom made for each individual client.

WHAT YOU CAN DO:

Ask your client what problems he really wants to change, then, come up with a statement about that problem. "I want to fight less with my wife." becomes the assessment item "I'm satisfied with how my wife and I are getting along." Then, provide a Likert-type ranking scale to measure the client's attitude and give the client the assessment as often as each session. Cap the custom assessment at about five questions. Here's an example of a simple custom assessment:

Instructions: Answer each question using the scale provided. Circle the number that matches how you feel about the statement.

	1	2	3	4	5
1. I am satisfied with how my wife and I are getting along.	(Strongly Disagree)	(Disagree)	(Neutral)	(Agree)	(Strongly Agree)
2. I am avoiding triggers effectively.	(Strongly Disagree)	(Disagree)	(Neutral)	(Agree)	(Strongly Agree)
3. I show up for work on time.	(Strongly Disagree)	(Disagree)	(Neutral)	(Agree)	(Strongly Agree)
4. I exercise five times per week for 30 minutes.	(Strongly Disagree)	(Disagree)	(Neutral)	(Agree)	(Strongly Agree)

5. I am completely free of all drug and alcohol use.

| 1 (Strongly Disagree) | 2 (Disagree) | 3 (Neutral) | 4 (Agree) | 5 (Strongly Agree) |

DESIRED OUTCOME:

Your client will have a visual representation of his progress on the items that matter most to him. You will have a measurement of how the client views his behavior on his custom items. You will be able to graph improvement, stagnation, or failure and you will be able to efficiently target problems and praise successes.

Substance Use & Alcohol
www.MyMSW.info

Lesson # 22

Part of the beauty of Motivational interviewing is its complex interconnections.

Once you begin to understand the basic concepts, you need to integrate the Stage of Changes.

There are five basic stages of change.

> Precontemplation
> Contemplation
> Preparation
> Action
> Maintenance
> Relapse (Not really a stage)

Let's go through the steps by first defining them; secondly looking at things to consider; third, the therapists tasks, and finally strategies and outcomes.

Definitions

Precontemplation Defined
People in precontemplation stage have no intention of changing their behavior for the foreseeable future. They are not thinking about changing their behavior, and may not see the behavior as a problem when asked. They certainly do not believe it is as problematic as external observers see it. These individuals are often labeled as "resistant" or in "denial."

Contemplation Defined
The person is aware a problem exists and seriously considers, action, but has not yet made a commitment to an action.

Preparation Defined
The person is intent upon taking action soon and often report some steps in that direction. Thus, this stage is a combination of behavioral actions and intentions. This is a relatively transitory stage that is characterized by the individual's making a firm commitment to the change process. There may already be some initial steps taken towards change, but even if not, most clients will make a serious attempt at change soon (i.e. one month).

Action Defined
The person is aware a problem exists and actively modifies their behavior, experiences and environment in order to overcome the problem. Commitment is clear and a great deal of effort is expended towards making changes.

Maintenance Defined
The person has made a sustained change wherein a new pattern of behavior has replaced the old. Behavior is firmly established and threat of relapse becomes less intense.

Relapse Defined
Falling back into old behaviors.

Things to Consider

Precontemplation - Things to Consider
Reasons for precontemplation can fit into the "four R's": reluctance, rebellion, resignation, and rationalization. DiClemente (1991) described why these groups do not consider change and methods for intervening.

Contemplation – Things to Consider
This is a paradoxical stage of change. The client is willing to consider the problem and possibility of change, yet ambivalence can make contemplation a chronic condition. Clients are quite open to information and yet wait for the one final piece of information that will compel them to change. It's almost as they either waits for a magic moment or an irresistible piece of information that will make the decision for them. This is a particularly opportune time for motivational interviewing strategies.

Contemplation and interest in change are not commitment. Information and incentives to change are important elements for assisting contemplators. Personally relevant information can have a strong impact at this stage.

Preparation - Things to Consider
Despite making a decision to alter behavior, change is not automatic. Ambivalence, though diminishing, is still present. The decision-making process is still occurring and pros and cons are still being weighed.

Action – Things to Consider
Action involves a sustained effort at making changes. This period usually lasts from one to six months. Clients have made a plan and have begun implementing it. Ambivalence and commitment are still issues. Too often people do not go back and re-evaluate their change plan. Where is it working? Where did it not? Is there a procedure for re-evaluating the plan? Has there been any planning for handling little slips? Recognize differing levels of readiness to change among issues and the recycling process in the Stages of Change

Maintenance - Things to consider
Maintenance is often viewed as an afterthought where very little activity occurs. However, maintenance is not a static stage. Relapse is possible and occurs for a variety of reasons. Most relapses are not automatic but occur after an initial slip has occurred. Clients will often turn to a therapist during what Saul Shiffman calls a relapse crisis (i.e., they've slipped or are about to). During these times the client's self-efficacy is weakened and fear is high. Clients seek reassurance from therapists while trying to make sense of the crisis. Review of the spiral model of the Stages of Change can be very helpful for clients at these times.

Therapist Tasks

Precontemplation - Therapist Tasks
- Identify "the problem" - this often means something different for the therapist and the client.
- Be aware of difference between reason and rationalization. A person, well aware of the risks and problems, may choose to

continue the behavior. We may not change them in the face of this informed choice. Our work may have an impact later.
- Recognize that more is not always better. More intensity will produce fewer results with this group.

Use MI strategies to raise awareness and doubt. Increase the client's perceptions of risks and problems with current behavior.
- Remember the goal is not to make precontemplators change immediately, but to help move them to contemplation.

Contemplation - Therapist Tasks
- Consider the pros and cons (from the clients perspective) of the problem behavior, as well as the pros and cons of change.
- Gather information about past change attempts. Frame these in terms of "some success" rather than change failures."
- Explore options the client has considered for the change process and offer additional options where indicated and if the client is interested. Remember that our clients are rarely novices to the change process.
- Elicit change statements.

Preparation - Therapist Tasks
- Assess strength of commitment. Strong verbal statements may be a sign of weak commitment. A realistic evaluation of problem area and a calm dedication to making this a top priority are good indicators
- Examine barriers and elicit solutions (what will the first week be like?)
- Build coping behaviors
- Reinforce commitment but provide words of caution where enthusiasm may outdistance actual skills

Action - Therapist Tasks
- Help increase client's self-efficacy by:
- Focusing on successful activity
- Reaffirming commitment
- Making intrinsic attributions for success

Maintenance - Therapist Tasks
Therapists do not usually see clients that are well-established in maintenance. If they do, a review of the action plan and a strategy for periodic review of the plan are useful. More often therapists will see clients when a relapse crisis is present. Tasks for these times are:
- Exploration of the factors precipitating and maintaining the crisis
- Provision of information
- Feedback about plans
- Empathy

Strategies and Outcomes

Precontemplation - Strategies
Primary tools are providing information and raising doubt. However, basic skills such as reflective listening, open-ended questions, and functioning as a collaborator (rather than an educator) may be enough. Matching interventions to the type of precontemplators is also helpful.

Precontemplation - Outcome
The client begins to consider that a problem or matter of concern exists.

Contemplation - Strategies
Inquire about the "good and less good" things of the problem behavior; explore concerns.

Contemplation - Outcome
The client is making change statements and makes a tentative commitment to changing the behavior.

Preparation - Strategies
Ask a key question. Assist client in building an action plan and removing barriers. Some examples of key questions are:
- What do you think you will do?
- What's the next step?
- It sounds like things can't stay how they are now. What are you going to do?

One structure for a change includes six elements:
- Specific statement of changes to be made
- Why these changes are important
- Steps in making these changes
- Inclusion of others in the plan
- A method for evaluating the plan • Identification of possible barriers to the plan

Preparation - Outcome
The client is making clear change statements and has an action plan in place.

Action - Strategies
This stage is familiar to most therapists and involves interventions they have experience in providing
(e.g. skill building, group work, relapse prevention, active problem solving, counter-conditioning, stimulus control, contingency management).

Action - Outcome
Clear changes in behavior are manifested and the risk of relapse diminishes as new behavior patterns replace the old problematic behavior.

Maintenance - Strategies
When crises are occurring, slow the process down. Explore what succeeded, as well as what is precipitating their current concerns or crisis. Offer models of success while normalizing relapse in situations where change is not easily accomplished. If the client is returning to discuss their success, reinforce their active efforts in making change possible and their commitment to change.

Maintenance - Outcome
Client exits the Stage of Change spiral. For a relapsing client, they re-enter the contemplation or preparation stage.

The Real World with Dan Knippel, LCSW

The Treatment Plan

PROBLEM:
The basic treatment plan is usually a written document that includes a statement of a ***problem***, a ***goal***, and the individual ***objectives*** that will help the client reach the goal.

A treatment plan is a metaphorical set of railroad tracks that guides the client to his desired outcome while minimizing drift, time-wasting, and aimless wandering. You want to help the client reach his goals, but how do you know you made it there without a plan?

WHAT YOU CAN DO:
Treatment plans should always be in the client's own words (not yours) and the goals and objectives should be SMART: **S**imple, **M**easurable, **A**chievable, **R**ealistic, and **T**imely. Treatment plans can have multiple problems and goals. Here is a basic example of a treatment plan:

Problem: *"I use weed and crack and it is hurting my relationships, is making me sick, and costs me money I need for other things."*
Goal #1: *"I will stop using weed by January 1st."*

> **Objective 1a**: *"I will attend counseling weekly."*
> **Objective 1a**: *"I will attend NA meetings on Tuesday and Saturday."*
> **Objective 1c**: *"I will remove my dealer's number from my phone."*
> **Objective 1d**: *"I will use Oak Street instead of Elm Street where my user friends live."*
> **Objective 1e**: *"I will make a list of at least 5 safe, non-user friends and family I am willing to hang out with."*

Goal #2: *"I will change my life so I do not resort to crack use again."*
> **Objective 2a**: *"I will write a list of the triggers to using crack and discuss them with my counselor."*

Objective 2b: *"I will direct deposit my paycheck into my wife's account."*

Objective 2c: *"I will only use a prepaid credit card and not carry any cash."*

Etcetera…

DESIRED OUTCOME:
Your client will have a "guide" that will keep him on track toward accomplishing his goal. A treatment plan allows you to use clinical skills to compliment the accomplishment of an objective. You might say, "You are really taking this seriously. You said you have been to four NA meetings a week for 5 weeks straight. That must feel good to be exceeding your objective." (Notice how *Objective 1a* was simple enough to be achieved and it was measurable so the client knows if he is accomplishing it or not.)

Good counseling should result in some sort of change that leaves the client closer to how he wants things to be (his goal) and farther away from how things are (his problem).

Believe it or not, some substance abuse counselors do not use treatment plans. Don't be one of them.

Substance Use & Alcohol
www.MyMSW.info

Lesson # 23

One of the primary acronyms used in MI is O.A.R.S.

This is a brief method of remembering the basic approached to using Motivational Interviewing in practice. They are sometimes called Micro-Counseling-Skills.

OARS stands for **Open Ended Questions, Affirmations, Reflections, and Summaries.**

These are:

Open-ended questions:
These are questions that make it difficult for a client to answer with a "Yes" or a "No". They also discourage clients from answering a questions with a short, specific, limited piece of information. These questions invite the client into the conversation and help them think about issues more deeply and with more elaboration. These questions also move the conversation forward and allow the client to explore reasons for change and the different possibilities for change. Closed-Ended questions have their place in an interview, but they can also stifle communication.

Affirmations:
These are statements that make communication better. They are statements that allow you to recognize you client's strengths. These statements allow you to build rapport with your client and help them see themselves in a different light. These statements are only effective when they are genuine. They must be congruent to be effective. Using an affirmation that does not match the client will often be perceived as superficial. Often clients have tried to change in the past and have been ineffective. Affirmations allow clients the chance to start again and to feel change is possible. These statements often reframe behaviors to show the client's positive qualities. These are the key element in facilitating MI's principle of Self-Efficacy.

Reflections
Of all the skills in MI, reflective listening is probably the most crucial skill. Reflective listening has two primary and crucial purposes. Its first purpose is to activate the basic principle of Expressing Empathy. When the therapist provides careful listening and appropriate reflective responses, the client will begin to accept that the therapist understands the issues from their perspective. Reflective listening also assists in guiding the client toward their change and supporting the client's goal-directed change. Reflections assist the client in perceiving their ambivalence and allow them to focus on the negative aspects of the status quo. It helps them focus on change.

Summaries:
These are a special form of a reflection in which the therapist reviews and recaps what has been discussed and decided in one or more of the counseling sessions. These reflections communicate interest, understanding and allow the therapist and client to identify the most important elements of the conversation. Summaries can be used to help the client re-frame and shift their attention in a new direction, thereby preparing them to change and "move on." These statements are able to highlight both sides of a client's ambivalence about change and promote the development of discrepancies that can be selected by the therapist to strategically determine which information needs to be augmented and which information should be minimized.

Change Talk
These are statements are made by the client. They enable to therapist to watch the client as they reveal the clients consideration and motivation and a commitment to change. The task of the therapist using MI seeks to guide the client to the expressions of change talk. The therapist is not the Guru. They are the trail-guide. Current research shows a clear correlation between client statements about change and the outcomes the client later reports. These reports show a greater level of success in changing a behavior. The more your client talks about change; the more likely they are to change.

Different types of change talk can be described using the mnemonic DARN---CAT.

Preparatory Change Talk
Desire (I want to change)
Ability (I can change)
Reason (It's important to change)
Need (I should change) and most predictive of positive outcome:
Implementing Change Talk

Commitment (I will make changes)
Activation (I am ready, prepared, willing to change)
Taking Steps (I am taking specific actions to change)

10 Strategies for Evoking Change Talk

These are the specific therapeutic strategies that are likely to elicit and support change talk in Motivational Interviewing:

1. Ask Evocative Questions: Ask an open question, the answer to which is likely to be change talk.

2. Explore Decisional Balance: Ask for the pros and cons of both changing and staying the same.

3. Good Things/Not---So---Good Things: Ask about the positives and negatives of the target behavior.

4. Ask for Elaboration/Examples: When a change talk theme emerges, ask for more details.

"In what ways?"
"Tell me more?"
"What does that look like?"
"When was the last time that happened?"

5. Look Back: Ask about a time before the target behavior emerged. How were things better, different?

6. Look Forward: Ask what may happen if things continue as they are (status quo). Try the miracle question:

If you were 100% successful in making the changes you want, what would be different?
How would you like your life to be five years from now?

7. Query Extremes: What are the worst things that might happen if you don't make this change? What are the best things that might happen if you do make this change?

8. Use Change Rulers:

Ask: "On a scale from 1 to 10, how important is it to you to change [the specific target behavior] where 1 is not at all important, and a 10 is extremely important?

Follow up: "And why are you at ___ and not _____ [a lower number than stated]?" "What might happen that could move you from ___ to [a higher number]?"

Alternatively, you could also ask: "How confident are that you could make the change if you decided to do it?"

9. Explore Goals and Values: Ask what the person's guiding values are. What do they want in life? Using a values card sort activity can be helpful here. Ask how the continuation of target behavior fits in with the person's goals or values. Does it help realize an important goal or value, interfere with it, or is it irrelevant?

10. Come Alongside: Explicitly side with the negative (status quo) side of ambivalence. "Perhaps _____ is so important to you that you won't give it up, no matter what the cost

The Real World with Dan Knippel, LCSW

Searching for Strengths.

PROBLEM:
By the time they get to you, many substance-abusing clients have caused serious damage to their finances, families, relationships; nearly every aspect of their lives has been marred. It may be hard for your client to find anything he considers a strength in his life. Identifying supports and strengths can sometimes foster a sense of hope and give direction.

WHAT YOU CAN DO:
Begin looking for strengths when you first meet the client and don't stop. Your job is to help identify strengths that can be exploited to meet his goals. Is he polite and well mannered? Did he shake your hand and smile when he greeted you? Does he speak clearly and properly? Does he have a job or is he motivated to go to work? Is he healthy? Does he accept assistance and utilize the community's resources effectively? Does his neighbor look out for him and drive him places? Look for:

- any supportive family member
- a boyfriend, girlfriend, or fiancé
- a home
- an adult child or responsible teenager
- the property manager or landlord
- any income, monthly check
- a phone, computer, internet service
- speaks clearly, uses

- a spouse
- a supportive ex-spouse
- any siblings
- a supportive neighbor
- any supportive friend
- any money in the bank or any cash asset
- dresses appropriately
- is polite and well

- proper language skills
- gets around by bicycle and bus pass
- food stamps, WIC
- a faith group or church
- health insurance
- mannered
- a case manager at a community agency
- a sense of humor
- AA or NA relationships, other groups
- hobbies or other pro-social leisure activity
- able to use the VA system, old career pension system, Social Security, Medicare, etc.
- able to use resources of a college or university

Finding strengths is like picking fruit from a tree. When you find a strength, pick it and place it in the basket to use later. Strengths may not always be easy to see and you may have to really reach for some of them, but you will find a few if you look hard enough.

QUESTION: Why do you think wearing clean, neat clothes, being well groomed, and speaking clearly while using proper language skills could be important strengths?

DESIRED OUTCOME:
You will be able to guide your client to use his strengths, resources, and supports to help him get closer to his goals.

Substance Use & Alcohol
www.MyMSW.info

Lesson # 24

What MI is...

Engagement - Building rapport:
- In MI the client-therapist relationship is in the forefront and it never left to chance or chemistry.
- The MI therapist begins by developing trust, building rapport, by providing the client with an empathic, reflective, sounding-board so they can hear what they say and feel heard.
- The MI therapist will follow the spirit of MI by expressing empathy, respecting autonomy, assisting collaboration, reflecting genuineness.
- The MI therapist will strive to create an atmosphere of safety and acceptance.
- The MI therapist is careful not to address topics too soon, which could cause therapist-client dissonance and harm the MI relationship.

Goal Directed:
- The MI therapist refers to identified goals, objectives and target behaviors.
- The MI therapist attains clarity, through engagement, about the target behavior or goal being addressed, and then strives to keep the discussion focused on these targets in order to keep the communication focused and productive.
- The MI therapist needs to be vigilant around the need to shift away from a topic when the client is expressing resistance or does not want to continue in this area.

The structure of a Goal-Directed discussion may be:
- The client begins by discussing developmental issues or historical concerns that may cause pain and distress.
- Once the discussion is complete, the MI therapist should begin to assist the client in discovering the relationship between the client's history and their present goals.

Resolve ambivalence:
- The MI therapist begins to facilitate the client's exploration of ambivalence, with a discussion that emphasizes change talk and 'tipping the balance' towards behavior change.
- The MI therapist begins to guide the client toward internal recognition about their behavior, whether their behavior is a problem, and helping the client reach a decision about change.

Menu of options:
- The MI therapist assists the client in referring to a numerous actions that the client and provider collaboratively identify and agree to include in a behavior change plan.
- The MI therapist uses a menu. This menu refers to the identification of six or seven specific actions that will be discussed.
- The MI therapist places emphasis on the client's willingness to pursue an identified action.
- The MI therapist will only include actions on the plan that the client is willing to pursue.
- The MI therapist will work with the client to assure the plan is fluid and capable of change.
- The MI therapist prioritizes each action is directed toward confidence building while conveying the hope that change can be attained.

Pros and Cons:
- The MI therapist uses this strategic intervention to assist with the exploration of the positive and negative experiences a client might have regarding a particular behavior.
- The MI therapist uses this technique to elicit change talk when a client may not have identified any disadvantages voluntarily.
- The MI therapist begins with an exploration of the positive experiences the client may have (This is known as "sustain talk") until a level of comfort is reached and then they move on to what is "not so good" about the behavior.
- The MI therapist assists the client, who is comfortable, to begin identifying elements of concern; either for the first time or in a way that is not resistant or guarded.

- The MI therapist should place more emphasis on guiding the client to change talk, rather than involving themselves in "sustain talk."
- The MI therapist should always be concerned that "sustain talk" may be reinforcing and deflect from change talk.

The Decision Balance -- *Not a required technique to practice MI* (Miller & Rollnick, 2009).
This technique is not MI. It has been used routinely by some MI practitioners as a "required technique", but is not formally recognized.

It is a form of identifying pros and cons within four quadrants.
> Quadrant A -- What is good about continuing the behavior.
> Quadrant C -- What is not good about changing the behavior.
> Quadrant B -- What is not good about continuing the behavior.
> Quadrant D -- What is good about changing the behavior.

Weight is given to Columns A+B as compared to columns C+D.
This technique currently has limited use in MI, because it offers little in the form of change talk.

Ask permission to give advice or information: **AKA**: Giving advice vs. Asking Permission.

> Giving Advice: "AA groups would be good for you."
> Asking permission: "Would you be interested in hearing my ideas about what might be useful?"
>> If the client says yes, the practitioner might recommend AA or make other suggestions.

> Providing an opportunity for the client to reject the suggestions: "How do you think this might work for you?"
>> This allows the client pursues action only in areas agreed upon.

> Giving Advice: "Read this information on the medication you are using."
> Asking permission: "Would you be interested in learning more about this medication?"

If yes, some written materials might be provided.

What MI is Not...
- MI is not based on the transtheoretical model - the stages of change. They are two discrete models, and neither one requires the other;
- MI is not a way to trick people to get them to do what they do not want to do;
- MI is not a technique; it is more complex and better understood as a communication method;
- MI is not the decision balance, this has been over utilized and misperceived as MI methodology;
- MI does not require assessment feedback, this design is specific to MET;
- MI is not a form of cognitive- behavior therapy, nothing is installed, rather MI elicits from people what is already there;
- MI is not just client-centered counseling, it departs by being goal oriented and having intentional direction towards change;
- MI is not easy, it involves a complex set of skills that are used flexibly;
- MI is not what you are already doing, learning MI requires training, supervised practice and feedback; MI is not a panacea, it is not meant to be a school of psychotherapy, rather it is a particular tool for addressing a specific problem.

Metaphors that can be used during an MI session...
- Ambivalence is a bit like having a committee inside your mind, with members who disagree on a proper course of action. (p. 7)
- The partnership...conversation is a bit like sitting together on a sofa while the person pages through a life photo album. (p. 16)
- Evocation...is like...drawing water from a well. (p. 21)
- Planning is the clutch that engages the engine of change talk. (p. 30)
- A simple reflection...is like an iceberg...it is limited to what shows above the water, the content that has actually been expressed, whereas a complex reflection makes a guess about what lies beneath the surface. (p. 58)
- Practice without feedback...is like...golfing in pitch-black darkness. (p. 59)

- A simple rhythm in MI is to ask an open question and then to reflect what the person says, perhaps two reflections per question, like a waltz. (p. 63)
- Summaries are...strands that are woven together into a fabric, a single piece that contains all of their colors. (p. 69)
- Summaries are like...seeing the forest instead of one tree at a time. (p. 69)
- The focus is a light on the horizon toward which you keep moving. (p. 99)
- MI is like dancing, moving together, in which you offer gentle guidance. (p. 103)
- The smallest glimmer of change talk may be a coal that if given some air will start to glow, becoming the fuel of change. (p. 103)
- Agenda mapping is like...examining a map at the outset of a journey. (p. 106)
- This approach [agenda mapping] is like looking at a map and seeing the places you might go, perhaps like two people on a sailboat slowing down for a moment to agree on a new course before catching the wind again. (p. 106)
- If the client's life is like a forest, agenda mapping involves soaring over it for a moment with the perspective of an eagle. (p. 107)
- Zooming in...is like pushing the plus (+) button to zoom in and get a better look at a particular area. (p. 108)
- Agenda mapping can be...a matter of listening to the client's story and puzzling together about a route out of the forest...where you may follow various streams to map the terrain (p. 116)
- The interviewer is keeping the whole picture in focus (eagle view) rather than zooming down to a particular task (mouse view). (p. 116)
- Change talk is a bit like walking up one side of a hill and down another. (p. 163)
- MI helps people out of the forest of ambivalence...MI helps them to keep moving from tree to tree until at last they find their way out of the forest. (p. 166)
- Early in an MI session the skill is often to discern a ray of change talk within the sustain talk, like spotting a lighthouse in a storm

- or detecting a signal within noise. It is not necessary to eliminate the storm or the noise, just follow the signal. (p. 178)
- Discord is like fire (or at least smoke) in the therapeutic relationship. (p. 197)
- Just as a smoke alarm alerts you to a change in the air, tune your ear to hear signals of dissonance and recognize them as important. (p. 204)
- MI is like improvisational theater. No two sessions run exactly the same way. (p. 211)
- As with motivation more generally, hope is evoked from within the client. The seeds of hope are already there, waiting to be uncovered and brought into the light. (p. 214)
- Be careful not to give in to the righting reflex...that will shut [clients] down like alligator jaws. (p. 249)
- Getting up on your soapbox tends to leave people with a soapy taste in the mouth. (p. 249)
- Sometimes it moves quickly, but engaging, focusing, and evoking can be a slow step-by-step process like snowshoeing up the side of a mountain. The progress may be steady, but it feels effortful, there are likely to be a few backslides, and you have to pay attention to where you are going. (p. 257)
- Planning...is more like a downhill ski...there is still the danger of running into trees, taking the wrong trail, or even heading off a cliff, so you still have to pay attention...(p. 257)
- Mobilizing change talk...is language on the far side of the ambivalence hill...(p. 285)
- You continue to explore the forest of change, moving from tree to tree in a reasonably straight line. Beneath the surface, seeds are germinating. (p. 289)
- It can feel comfortable to take the lead [in a conversation], confident in one's expertise, and it can also quite soon feel frustrating—a bit like pulling someone across the dance floor, trips and all. (p. 310)
- Learning MI is like learning to fly an airplane...it is an on-going process and more than knowledge is involved. (p. 322)
- Feedback is fundamental...It is difficult to learn archery in the dark. (p. 323)
- Can you do MI in a few minutes? It is in a way like asking, Can you play the piano for 5 minutes? (p. 343)

- Low-quality MI practice might be likened to half-doses of a vaccine or antibiotic: the right idea but insufficient strength. (p. 351)
- An MI trainer should...be able to demonstrate it competently on the spot. It would be a rare violin teacher who cannot play the instrument competently. (p. 354).
- While we hold a parental fondness for this growing child that we have nurtured, and entertain some worries for its future development, we have come far enough together to stand back in wonderment and curiosity to see what will happen next. (p. 402)

Motivational Interviewing, Third Edition: Helping People Change (Applications of Motivational Interviewing) William R. Miller, Stephen Rollnick. The Guilford Press; Third Edition (September 7, 2012)

A FANTASTIC MI Resource --- http://www.motivationalinterview.org

The Real World with Dan Knippel, LCSW

Resist the Urge to Be the Expert.

PROBLEM:
Sometimes the therapist cannot resist the urge to be helpful and direct the client's therapeutic goals. If you're like everyone else, you resist change when people tell you what you *need* to do or what you *should* do. Once, a counselor told his client, "You know you're hurting your family by your actions. You need to stop hanging out with your drinking buddy and you should start going to AA meetings." Another client waited weeks to confide in his counselor about a pornography habit. The counselor said, "Well the first thing you need to do is stop looking at that." Neither client ever returned. Clients should feel comfortable with the pace and direction of their own therapeutic process. They do best when using their own internal skills and knowledge to find solutions that work best for them. Resist the urge to tell the client what to do. Resist the urge to fix their problems. Instead, ask the client what he wants to do next.

WHAT YOU CAN DO:
Test the waters. You may have a really good idea of what the client's problems are and how they could be fixed. Instead of giving advice, test the waters by asking where he is at in his own change process.
Which of the following is the best response to the client?

Client: "It's not every single day, but I have been drinking way more than I used to. I only drink when I hang out with my two friends after work. I can see that it could become a real problem if I don't stop, and, I guess I'm afraid I might go off the deep end and not be able to stop drinking if I don't do something soon."

    A. "You're concerned about how things are going. Do you mind if I ask you something? You said you think stopping might be the best thing for you, but whatever you do is your choice. What do you want to do next?"

B. "You know what you need to do? You need to stop hanging out with those guys after work and just go home. You should go to AA meetings, too, because you're going to need a sponsor."

Answer: A

DESIRED OUTCOME:
Using answer "A" above, you are giving the client the chance to think things through and you are testing the waters to see what he is ready for. Maybe he is afraid of how he'll feel physically if he stops drinking. Maybe he wants to talk about ways to deal with pressure to drink. Maybe he is drinking to cope with something going on at home. He can address the things he wants to and choose the pace and focus of counseling. Then, change happens because he is ready, not because you told him to.

APPENDIX A

CLINICAL INSITUTUE WITHDRAWAL ASSESSMENT OF ALCOHOL SCALE, REVISED (CIWA-AR)

According to Sullivan(1989), the CIWA-Ar scale can measure 10 symptoms. Scores of less than 8 to 10 indicate minimal to mild withdrawal. Scores of 8 to 15 indicate moderate withdrawal (marked autonomic arousal); and scores of 15
or more indicate severe withdrawal (impending *delirium tremens*). The assessment requires 2 minutes to perform (Sullivan, et al, 1989).

NAUSEA AND VOMITING — Ask "Do you feel sick to your stomach? Have you vomited?" <u>Observation.</u>
    0 no nausea and no vomiting
    1 mild nausea with no vomiting
    2
    3
    4 intermittent nausea with dry heaves
    5
    6
    7 constant nausea, frequent dry heaves and vomiting

TREMOR — Arms extended and fingers spread apart. <u>Observation.</u>
    0 no tremor
    1 not visible, but can be felt fingertip to fingertip
    2
    3
    4 moderate, with patient's arms extended
    5
    6
    7 severe, even with arms not extended

PAROXYSMAL SWEATS — <u>Observation</u>.
    0 no sweat visible
    1 barely perceptible sweating, palms moist
    2
    3
    4 beads of sweat obvious on forehead
    5
    6
    7 drenching sweats

ANXIETY — Ask "Do you feel nervous?" <u>Observation.</u>
- 0 no anxiety, at ease
- 1 mild anxious
- 2
- 3
- 4 moderately anxious, or guarded, so anxiety is inferred
- 5
- 6
- 7 equivalent to acute panic states as seen in severe delirium or acute schizophrenic reactions

AGITATION — <u>Observation.</u>
- 0 normal activity
- 1 somewhat more than normal activity
- 2
- 3
- 4 moderately fidgety and restless
- 5
- 6
- 7 paces back and forth during most of the interview, or constantly thrashes about

TACTILE DISTURBANCES — Ask "Have you any itching, pins and needles sensations, any burning, any numbness, or do you feel bugs crawling on or under your skin?" <u>Observation.</u>
- 0 none
- 1 very mild itching, pins and needles, burning or numbness
- 2 mild itching, pins and needles, burning or numbness
- 3 moderate itching, pins and needles, burning or numbness
- 4 moderately severe hallucinations
- 5 severe hallucinations
- 6 extremely severe hallucinations
- 7 continuous hallucinations

AUDITORY DISTURBANCES — Ask "Are you more aware of sounds around you? Are they harsh? Do they frighten you? Are you hearing anything that is disturbing to you? Are you hearing things you know are not there?" <u>Observation.</u>
- 0 not present
- 1 very mild harshness or ability to frighten
- 2 mild harshness or ability to frighten
- 3 moderate harshness or ability to frighten
- 4 moderately severe hallucinations
- 5 severe hallucinations
- 6 extremely severe hallucinations
- 7 continuous hallucinations

VISUAL DISTURBANCES — Ask "Does the light appear to be too bright? Is its color different? Does it hurt your eyes? Are you seeing anything that is disturbing to you? Are you seeing things you know are not there?" <u>Observation.</u>

0 not present
1 very mild sensitivity
2 mild sensitivity
3 moderate sensitivity
4 moderately severe hallucinations
5 severe hallucinations
6 extremely severe hallucinations
7 continuous hallucinations

HEADACHE, FULLNESS IN HEAD — Ask "Does your head feel different? Does it feel like there is a band around your head?"
Do not rate for dizziness or lightheadedness. Otherwise, rate severity.

0 no present
1 very mild
2 mild
3 moderate
4 moderately severe
5 severe
6 very severe
7 extremely severe

Ask "What day is this? Where are you? Who am I?"

0 oriented and can do serial additions
1 cannot do serial additions or is uncertain about date
2 disoriented for date by no more than 2 calendar days
3 disoriented for date by more than 2 calendar days
4 disoriented for place/or person

The Clinical Institute Withdrawal Assessment - Alcohol (CIWA-A) and a shortened version, the CIWA-A revised (CIWA-Ar). This scale has well documented reliability, reproducibility and validity, based on comparison to ratings by expert clinicians (Knott, et al, 1981; Wiehl, et al 1994; Sullivan, et al, 1989). From 30 signs and symptoms, the scale has been carefully refined to a list of 10 signs and symptoms in the CIWA-Ar (Wiehl, et al, 1994). It is thus easy to use and has been shown to be feasible to use in a variety of clinical settings, including detoxification units (Naranjo, et al, 1983; Hoey, et al, 1994), psychiatry units (Heinala, et al, 1990), and general medical/surgical wards (Young, et al, 1987; Katta, 1991). The CIWA-Ar has added usefulness because high scores, in addition to indicating severe withdrawal, are also predictive of the development of seizures and delirium (Naranjo, et al, 1983; Young, et al, 1987).

For Benzodiazapines

The instrument also has been adapted for benzodiazepine withdrawal assessment (Clinical Institute Withdrawal Assessment-Benzodiazepine).

A study of the revised version of the CIWA predicted that those with a score of >15 were at increased risk for severe alcohol withdrawal (RR 3.72;95% confidence interval 2.85-4.85); the higher the score, the greater the risk. Some patients (6.4%) still suffered complications, despite low scores, if left untreated (Foy, et al, 1988).

> *The CIWA-Ar is not copyrighted and may be reproduced freely. Sullivan, J.T.; Sykora, K.; Schneiderman, J.; Naranjo, C.A.; and Sellers, E.M. Assessment of alcohol withdrawal: The revised Clinical Institute Withdrawal Assessment for Alcohol scale (CIWA-Ar). British Journal of Addiction 84:1353-1357, 1989.*

REFERENCES

American Psychiatric Association. (1994). *Diagnostic and statistical manual of mental disorders* (4th ed., text rev.). Washington, DC: Author.

American Association of Suicidology. (2007.) *U.S.A. Suicide: 2007 Official Final Data.* Available at http://www.suicidology.org/c/document_library/get_file?folderId=232&name=DLFE-232.pdf. Last accessed December 16, 2013.

Astry, C.L., Warr, G.A., & Jakab, G.J. (1983). Impairment of poly-morphonuclear leukocyte immigration as a mechanism of alcohol-induced suppression of pulmonary antibacterial defenses. *American Review of Respiratory Disease, 128(1),* 113-117.

Bassetti, C., & Aldrich MS. Alcohol consumption and sleep apnea in patients with TIA and ischemic stroke. *Journal of Sleep Research, 25,* 400.

Bertrand, J., Floyd, R.L., Weber, M.K., et al. (2004). *National Task Force on FAS/FAE. Fetal Alcohol Syndrome: Guidelines for Referral and Diagnosis.* Atlanta, GA: Centers for Disease Control and Prevention.

Black, M. (1984). Acetaminophen hepatotoxicity. *Annual Review of Medicine, 35,* 577-593.

Cadoret, R.J., Yates, W.R., Troughton, E., Woodworth, G., & Stewart, M.A. (1995). Adoption study demonstrating two genetic pathways to drug abuse. *Archives of General Psychiatry, 52,* 42-52.

Chambers, J.C., Ueland, P.M., & Obeid, O.A. (2000). Improved vascular endothelial function after oral B vitamins: an effect mediated through reduced concentrations of free plasma homocysteine. *Circulation, 102,* 2479-2483.

Conrod, P.J., Pihl, R.O., & Ditto, B. (1995). Autonomic reactivity and alcohol-induced dampening in men at risk for alcoholism and men at risk for hypertension. *Alcoholism: Clinical and Experimental Research, 19,* 482-489.

Cornelius, J.R., Salloum, I.M., Day, N.L., Thase, M.E., & Mann, J.J. (1996). Patterns of suicidality and alcohol use in alcoholics with major depression. *Alcoholism: Clinical and Experimental Research, 20,* 1451-1455.

Department of Health and Human Services and U.S. Department of Agriculture (USDA). (2000). *Nutrition and Your Health: Dietary Guidelines for Americans.* (5th ed.).

Home and Garden Bulletin No. 232. Washington, DC: USDA.

Dhar, S., Omran, L., Bacon, B.R., Solomon, H., & Di Bisceglie, A.M. (1994). Liver transplantation in patients with chronic hepatitis C and alcoholism. *Digestive Diseases and Sciences, 44,* 2003-2007.

Dufour, M.C. (1999). What Is Moderate Drinking? Defining "drinks" and drinking levels. *Alcohol Research and Health, 23,* 5-14.

Feinman, L. (1989). Absorption and utilization of nutrients in alcoholism. *Alcohol Health & Research World, 13,* 207-210.

Girre, C., Hispard, E., Palombo, S., N'Guyen, C., & Dally, S. (1993). Increased metabolism of acetaminophen in chronically alcoholic patients. *Alcoholism: Clinical and Experimental Research, 17,* 170-173.

Goodwin, D.W., Schulsinger, F., Moller N, et al. (1974). Drinking problems in adopted and non-adopted sons of alcoholics. *Archives of General Psychiatry, 31,* 164-169.

Grant, B.F., Stinson, F.S., & Harford, T.C. (2001). Age at onset of alcohol use and DSM-IV alcohol abuse and dependence: a 12-year follow-up. *Journal of Substance Abuse, 13,* 493-504.

Holdstock, L., & de Wit, H. (1998). Individual differences in the biphasic effects of ethanol. *Alcoholism: Clinical and Experimental Research, 22,* 1903-1911.

Graham, A.W., & Fleming, M.S. (1998). Brief interventions. In Graham, A.W., Schultz, T.K., & Wilford, B.B. (Eds.), *Principles of Addiction Medicine.* (2nd ed.) (pp. 615-630). Chevy Chase, MD: American Society of Addiction Medicine, Inc.

Hall, P. (1995). Factors influencing individual susceptibility to alcoholic liver disease. In Hall, P. (Ed), *Alcoholic Liver Disease: Pathology and Pathogenesis,* (2nd ed.). (pp. 299-316). London: Edward Arnold.

Hagedorn, J.C., Encarnacion, B., Brat, G.A., & Morton, J.M. (2007). Does gastric bypass alter alcohol metabolism? *Surgery for Obesity and Related Diseases, 3,* 543-548.

Holdstock, L., de Wit, H. (2001). Individual differences in responses to ethanol and d-amphetamine: a within-subject study. *Alcoholism: Clinical and Experimental Research, 25,* 540-548.

Ewing, J.A. (1984). Detecting Alcoholism: The CAGE Questionnaire. *Journal of the American Medical Association, 252,* 1905-1907.

Korsten, M.A. (1989). Alcoholism and pancreatitis: Does nutrition play a role? *Alcohol Health & Research World, 13,* 232-237.

King, A.C., Houle, T., de Wit, H., Holdstock, L., & Schuster, A. (2002). Biphasic alcohol response differs in heavy versus light drinkers. *Alcoholism: Clinical and Experimental Research, 26,* 827-835.

Lapham, S.C., Smith, E., C'de Baca, J., et al. (2001). Prevalence of psychiatric disorders among persons convicted of driving while impaired. *Archives of General Psychiatry, 58,* 943-949.

Mann, J.J. (2002). A current perspective of suicide and attempted suicide. *Annals of Internal Medicine, 136,* 302-311.

Moses, S. (n.d.). Lab Markers of Malnutrition. Available at http://www.fpnotebook.com/ Pharm/Lab/LbMrkrsOfMlntrtn.htm. Last accessed May 7, 2013.

Murphy, G.E., & Wetzel, R.D. (1990). The lifetime risk of suicide in alcoholism. *Archives of General Psychiatry, 47,* 383-392.

National Institute on Alcohol Abuse and Alcoholism. (1997). *Alcohol Alert No. 35: Alcohol Metabolism. PH 371.* Available at http://pubs.niaaa.nih.gov/publications/aa35.htm. Last accessed April 14, 2011.

Kenneth L. Davis, K.L., Charne, D., Coyle, J.T., & Nemeroff, C. (Eds.) (2002). *Neuropsychopharmacology: The Fifth Generation of Progress.* Philadelphia, PA: Lippincott Williams & Wilkins.

Knight, U.S. JR., Wechsler, H., Kuo, M., et al. (2002). Alcohol abuse and dependence among U.S. college students. *Journal of Studies on Alcohol and Drugs, 63,* 263-270.

MacGregor, R.R. (1986). Alcohol and immune defense. *Journal of the American Medical Association, 256,* 1474-1479.

Menz, V., Grimm, W., Hoffmann, J., & Maisch, B. (1996). Alcohol and rhythm disturbance: the holiday heart syndrome. *Herz, 21,* 227-231.

Mangoni, A.A., & Jackson, S.H. (2002). Homocysteine and cardiovascular disease: current evidence and future prospects. *American Journal of Medicine, 112,* 556-565.

Nakken, C. (1988, 1996). *The Addictive Personality: Understanding the addictive process and compulsive behavior.* Center City, MN: Hazelden.

National Council on Alcoholism and Drug Dependence of the San Fernado Valley. "Michigan Alcohol Screening Test (MAST)." Retrieved July 2007.

National Institute on Alcohol Abuse and Alcoholism. (1998). *Alcohol Alert No. 42. Alcohol and the Liver: Research Update.* Available at http://pubs.niaaa.nih.gov/publications/aa42.htm.

Preuss, U.W., Schuckit, M.A., & Smith, T.L. (2002). Comparison of 3190 alcohol-dependent individuals with and without suicide attempts. *Alcoholism: Clinical and Experimental Research, 26,* 471-477.

Regier, D.A., Farmer, M.E., Rae, D.S., et al. (1990). Comorbidity of mental disorders with alcohol and other drug abuse. *Journal of the American Medical Association, 264,* 2511-2518.

Resnick, M.D., Bearman, P.S., Blum, R.W., et al. (1997). Protecting adolescents from harm: findings from the National Longitudinal Study on Adolescent Health. *Journal of the American Medical Association, 278,* 823-832.

Sato, M., & Lieber, C.S. (1981). Hepatic vitamin A depletion after chronic ethanol consumption in baboons and rats. *Journal of Nutrition 111,* 2015-2023.

Substance Abuse and Mental Health Services Administration. (2010). *Results from the 2009 National Survey on Drug Use and Health. Volume I.* Rockville, MD: U.S. Department of Health and Human Services.

Schuckit, M.A. (2000). *Drug and Alcohol Abuse: A Clinical Guide to Diagnosis and Treatment.* (5th ed.). New York, NY: Kluwer Academic/Plenum Publishers.

Schuckit, M.A. Vulnerability factors for alcoholism. Kenneth L. Davis, K.L., Charne, D., Coyle, J.T., & Nemeroff, C. (Eds.) (2002). *Neuropsychopharmacology: The Fifth Generation of Progress.* Philadelphia, PA: Lippincott Williams & Wilkins.

Schoppet, M., & Maisch, B. (2001). Alcohol and the heart. *Herz, 26,* 345-352.

Schuck, A.M., & Widom, C.S. (2001). Childhood victimization and alcohol symptoms in females: causal inferences and hypothesized mediators. *Child Abuse & Neglect, 25,* 1069-1092.

Schuckit, M.A., Mazzanti, C., Smith, T.L., et al. (1999). Selective genotyping for the role of 5-HT2A, 5-HT2C, and GABA alpha 6 receptors and the serotonin transporter in the level of response to alcohol: a pilot study. *Biological Psychiatry, 45,* 647-651.

Soderpalm, A.H., De Wit, H. (2002). Effects of stress and alcohol on subjective state in humans. *Alcoholism: Clinical and Experimental Research, 26,* 818-826.

Stermer, E. (2002). Alcohol consumption and the gastrointestinal tract. *Israel Medical Association Journal, 4,* 200-202.

Stinson, F.S., & DeBakey, S.F. (1992). Alcohol-related mortality in the United States, 1979-1988. *British Journal of Addiction, 87,* 777-783.

Substance Abuse and Mental Health Services Administration. (2010). *Results from the 2009 National Survey on Drug Use and Health. Volume I.* Rockville, MD: U.S. Department of Health and Human Services.

Sullivan, M.A., & Rudnik-Levin, F. (2001). Attention deficit/hyperactivity disorder and substance abuse: Diagnostic and therapeutic considerations. *Annals of the New York Academy of Sciences, 931,* 251-270.

Thomson, A.D. (2000). Mechanisms of vitamin deficiency in chronic alcohol misusers and the development of the Wernicke-Korsakoff syndrome. *Alcohol, 35,* 2-7.

Thomson, A.D., & Pratt, O.E. (1992). Interaction of nutrients and alcohol: Absorption, transport, utilization, and metabolism. In Watson, R.R., & Watzl, B. (Eds.), *Nutrition and Alcohol.* Boca Raton, FL: CRC Press. pp. 75-99.

Trevisan, L.A., Boutros, N., Petrakis, I.L., & Krystal, J.H. (1998). Compilations Of Alcohol Withdrawal: Pathophysiological Insights. *Alcohol Health & Research World, 22,* 61-66.

Volavka, J., Czobor, P., Goodwin, D.W., et al. (1996). The electroencephalogram after alcohol administration in high-risk men and the development of alcohol use disorders 10 years later. *Archives of General Psychiatry, 53,* 258-263.

Van den Berg, H., van der Gaag, M., Hendriks, H. (2002). Influence of lifestyle on vitamin bioavailability. *International Journal for Vitamin and Nutrition Research, 72,* 53-59.

Zhang, P., Bagby, G.J., Happel, K.I., Summer, W.R., & Nelson, S. (2002). Pulmonary host defenses and alcohol. *Frontiers in Bioscience, 7,* 1314-d1330.

Vitiello, M.V. (1997). Sleep, alcohol and alcohol abuse. *Addiction Biology, 2,* 151-158.

Zambon, P., Talamini, R., La Vecchia, C., Dal Maso, L., et al. (2000). Smoking, type of alcoholic beverage and squamous-cell oesophageal cancer in northern Italy. *International Journal of Cancer, 86,* 144-149.

Made in the USA
Charleston, SC
12 December 2014